LISA G.A

" I've learned that transformation, inside and out, starts with taking that first step toward change, no matter how daunting it may seem. And for anyone out there struggling, remember, it's not just about losing weight— it's about gaining a whole new way of life."

Welcome to the Galveston Diet

Embarking on the Galveston Diet is like opening a new chapter in your book of life. It's a promise of transformation, where you step into a balanced lifestyle that harmonizes your body's needs with your aspirations for health and vitality. As you flip through these pages, you're not just reading a diet book; you're beginning a journey that could redefine your understanding of nutrition, wellness, and yourself.

This book introduces the Galveston Diet, a program distinct from the fleeting trends that saturate our culture. It's more than a mere regimen—it's a blueprint for a sustainable, wholesome lifestyle. The Galveston Diet doesn't revolve around harsh restrictions or exhaustive food logging. Instead, it focuses on nourishing your body with foods that combat inflammation, which is often the silent adversary behind weight gain and health issues.

Each chapter of this book is designed to guide you through understanding how your body processes food, the importance of hormonal balance, and the significant role inflammation plays in your overall health. By the end of this journey, you won't just be following a diet; you'll be equipped with the knowledge to make informed decisions that sustain your health long-term.

Consider the story of Sarah, a composite of the many real-life success stories that have been born from this diet. Like many of us, Sarah struggled to find balance in her hectic life, her health sitting quietly in the backseat. However, with the Galveston Diet, she didn't just lose weight—she gained energy, clarity, and a renewed sense of vitality. Her transformation was profound, not just physically but emotionally and psychologically.

The Galveston Diet is rooted in the science of anti-inflammatory foods, which are pivotal in turning the tide against chronic health issues. This diet emphasizes the importance of whole, nutrient-rich foods that restore and rejuvenate your body, not deplete it. You'll learn why certain foods have been included and how they contribute to your health, alongside practical advice on how to integrate these principles into your everyday life with ease.

Moreover, this book dispels the myths surrounding dietary fats, carbs, and proteins. It offers a fresh perspective on balancing macronutrients, aligning with your body's natural needs rather than against them. You'll discover recipes that aren't just healthy but are also delicious and satisfying, breaking the stereotype that healthy food must be bland or unappealing.

In preparing to write this book, I delved into the latest research, consulted experts, and refined the diet to ensure it's based on the most up-to-date scientific understanding. The Galveston Diet is a testament to the power of informed dietary choices and their impact on our health.

As you make your way through the Galveston Diet, you'll encounter strategies to overcome common pitfalls and challenges in maintaining a healthy diet. The book provides tools and tips to handle social situations, dining out, and high-stress periods without falling back into old habits.

Importantly, this diet is a journey towards self-discovery. It encourages you to listen to your body, understand its signals, and respond with love and care. It's about creating a sustainable relationship with food that celebrates your body's needs and your personal preferences.

In closing, I invite you to embrace this journey with an open heart and a willing spirit. The path laid out in this book isn't just about losing weight—it's about gaining a richer, more vibrant life. The Galveston Diet is here not only to guide you to your goals but to empower you to redefine what health means for you.

Together, let's step boldly into a future where your energy is boundless, your body is nourished, and your mind is clear. Welcome to a new you, welcome to the Galveston Diet—where your best self awaits.

TABLE OF CONTENTS

01

LISTEN

ACTION

02

03

CHAPTER ONE
LISTEN

My Story

After my breakup, life seemed to spiral out of control. The routines and habits I had built around the relationship fell apart, and in their place, I found myself turning to food and nightlife for solace. Clubbing until the early hours and indulging in one too many comfort meals became my new normal. Just over a month into this lifestyle, I gained over 18 pounds. It hit me hard one evening when I tried to pull on my favorite jeans and couldn't get them past my thighs. Even more alarming was that each night, it became harder to breathe as I lay in bed, my thoughts consumed by what I would eat next.

I knew I needed a change but felt utterly lost on how to begin. That was until I stumbled upon an article about the Galveston diet. Intrigued by its promise of not just weight loss but a sustainable approach to eating, I decided to give it a shot.

The Galveston diet focused on the importance of macros—proteins, fats, and carbohydrates—and the role of anti-inflammatory foods. This was not just about eating less but eating right. The learning curve was steep. Initially, I struggled to understand how to balance my meals, spending nights reading and days experimenting with new recipes that fit the diet's guidelines. Slowly, the fog began to lift. I learned to replace high-carb comfort foods with healthier alternatives and discovered I could still enjoy my favorite dishes by tweaking the ingredients to fit my macros.

A few months into this new way of life, the results were undeniable. Not only did I shed the extra weight, but my energy levels skyrocketed. I was no longer gasping for breath at night but sleeping peacefully. My thoughts were no longer fixated on food all day; instead, I enjoyed planning my meals and calculating my daily intake of macros, which had become second nature to me.

As I regained my shape and confidence, my perspective on life began to shift. I replaced my clubbing nights with gym sessions and cooking classes. The more I shared my journey on social media, the more I realized how many people were struggling with similar issues.

Now, a year later, I stand not only physically healthier but emotionally and mentally stronger. The breakup that once seemed like the end of my world was actually the beginning of a deeper, more meaningful journey toward self-discovery and health.

THE RIGHT
WAY TO EAT

2 "MEALS" + 2 "SNACKS" = 1 DAY

In my latest exploration of eating patterns, I discovered the Galveston Diet, which completely revolutionized my approach to traditional meal timings. The conventional labels of breakfast, lunch, and dinner have faded from my vocabulary, replaced by a more fluid concept of main meals and snacks throughout the day. This transformative approach not only simplifies eating but also aligns more naturally with our bodies' needs for sustained energy and metabolic health.

When you adopt the Galveston Diet, you shift from eating by the clock to eating by your body's cues. It's about understanding your hunger and fullness signals rather than adhering to socially prescribed meal times. Each day is structured around main meals and strategic snacks tailored to fuel your body efficiently. This method ensures that you continuously nourish your body with what it needs, when it needs it, without the arbitrary constraints of traditional meal times.

The Galveston Diet encourages a flexible eating schedule that can be incredibly liberating. For instance, if your day starts early, your first main meal might be at 9 AM, followed by a snack at noon, another main meal at 3 PM, and a final snack around 6 PM. This structure keeps your metabolism active and avoids the energy dips and peaks that are often associated with the standard three-meals-a-day regimen.

To illustrate the practicality and humor that can come with this new way of eating, I often share a personal anecdote. Once, when my best friend invited me to a traditional dinner, I playfully responded that I no longer recognized the term "dinner." This was not just a joke but a reflection of how deeply my eating habits had changed. The concept of 'dinner' implies a specific meal at a specific time, but on the Galveston Diet, what matters more is responding to your body's needs rather than clock-bound conventions.

Adopting this diet does require a shift in mindset. It would help if you became adept at planning your meals and snacks in a way that suits your daily energy requirements and lifestyle preferences. This might include preparing nutrient-dense foods in advance or choosing snacks that are satisfying and beneficial to your health. The focus is on balance and flexibility, ensuring you consume various daily nutrients to support overall well-being.

Moreover, this approach to eating encourages a better relationship with food. It moves away from the guilt and stress often associated with missing traditional meals or eating at 'wrong' times. Instead, it promotes an understanding that nourishing your body is a fluid, ongoing process that should adapt to the rhythms of your life, not the other way around.

In conclusion, the Galveston Diet isn't just about changing what you eat; it's about transforming how you think about eating. By breaking down the traditional meal structure and focusing on main meals and snacks based on your body's natural cues, you embrace a more intuitive and health-focused lifestyle. This way of eating can lead to significant improvements in energy levels, metabolic health, and overall quality of life.

How Should I Fast?

Incorporating fasting into your lifestyle can be a transformative but challenging process. I understand that altering your eating habits is not an easy task, so I advocate for a gradual approach to help ease the transition. From personal experience, I know the importance of making incremental changes to prevent overwhelming your body and maintain discipline in your new eating schedule.

For those new to the concept of intermittent fasting, it involves alternating cycles of eating and fasting. I personally follow the 16:8 method, which consists of consuming all my meals and snacks within an eight-hour window each day, from 8 AM to 4 PM, followed by 16 hours of fasting. This approach allows the body to enter a state of fasting long enough to burn through excess fat but is limited enough to be manageable during waking hours.

Adjusting to this schedule wasn't immediate—it took me over three weeks to adapt fully. If you are considering this method, start with a fasting interval that feels doable; for instance, begin with a 12:12 or 14:10 ratio, where you fast for 12 or 14 hours and eat during the remaining 12 or 10 hours of the day. Gradually increase the fasting period as your body adapts. This step-by-step increase helps manage hunger more effectively and prepares your body for longer fasting intervals.

A crucial aspect of fasting, and one that should not be overlooked, is hydration. During fasting periods, it's vital to stay hydrated. Water is your best friend, but you can also drink unsweetened tea and black coffee. These beverages help curb appetite slightly and keep you hydrated without breaking the fast.

The goal of adjusting meal times gradually is to align your body's internal clock to your new eating schedule without causing distress or discomfort. For example, if you find yourself eating dinner past 8 PM, try to eat a little earlier the next day, say around 7:45 PM, and gradually earlier each day until you reach your desired meal time. It is important not to adjust your meal times by more than 20 minutes from one day to the next to allow your stomach to adapt without discomfort.

By following these steps, you can make the transition to intermittent fasting smoother and more sustainable. Remember, discipline in maintaining your eating and fasting windows is key to success. As you adapt, you will notice significant improvements in both your physical and mental well-being, making the initial effort well worth it. Stick with it, stay hydrated, and watch as your body adapts and thrives in response to your new eating pattern.

My meal plan

Understanding the distribution of macros—fats, proteins, and carbohydrates—is critical, and I began by focusing predominantly on fat, maintaining its ratio at 60-75% of my daily intake, with proteins and carbs sharing the remaining 15-20%, usually around 20% each.

Assuming that every day, the ratio of fat + protein + carb = 100%, then, in one week, I will have the ratio of fat + protein + carb equal to 700%; you should aim for 500% fat during the first week. The remaining macros (proteins and carbs) are then split evenly. This high-fat approach is essential to gradually transitioning your body to metabolize fats more efficiently.

In the second week, the percentage of fats is slightly reduced to 495%. The percentage removed from fats is added to carbohydrates. This adjustment helps slowly re-introduce and increase carbs in the diet, aiding your body in adapting without significant shocks. It's vital during this phase to select new foods that cater to your personal taste preferences, and I recommend creating a personalized list of such foods and recipes before starting the process.

By the third week, I further decrease the fat percentage to 490% while continuing the incremental increase in carbs by another 5%. This gradual reduction and reallocation continue weekly, allowing the body to adapt progressively. By the fifth week, the fat macros percentage is brought down to 475%, with a corresponding increase in carbohydrates, which now make up more than 75% of the weekly macros percentages.

This approach not only makes the diet sustainable by allowing the inclusion of a variety of foods but also ensures that you don't feel overly hungry or too full. It's all about finding that perfect balance where your body feels satisfied throughout the day. Over the subsequent weeks, as I continued with this regimen, I noticed a significant drop in my weight. Moreover, I became adept at quickly finding and measuring the macro content before consuming any food, making it easier to stick to this diet with every meal.

This method teaches you to intuitively manage your eating habits based on macros calculations, ensuring a healthier lifestyle that is adaptable to your personal tastes and needs. By learning to adjust and balance your intake of fats, proteins, and carbohydrates, you set the stage for sustained health and weight management, which is why this detailed guide on macros counting is a fundamental part of the diet plan I share in my book.

Maintain

Maintaining weight after a successful weight loss journey is an ongoing process that requires continuous attention and adaptation. The transition from losing weight to maintaining it brings about a new set of challenges, but with the right approach, you can sustain your hard-earned results and continue to thrive healthily. Here's how to effectively maintain weight, balance nutrition, and ensure that the pounds you've shed do not creep back.

Understanding the Maintenance Phase

Weight maintenance is not simply a continuation of weight loss. Instead, it requires a deliberate shift in focus from weight reduction to nutritional balance and lifestyle management. When you enter the maintenance phase, your body's energy needs to adjust. The goal is to consume enough calories to provide your body with the fuel it needs without tipping the scale back up.

Finding the Right Macronutrient Balance

My own experience with weight maintenance involved adjusting the macronutrient composition of my diet—specifically, reducing fat intake and increasing carbohydrates. This balance might vary from person to person, but what worked for me was adhering to a macronutrient ratio of 40% fat, 20% protein, and 40% carbohydrates. This ratio supported not only my energy levels throughout the day but also helped stabilize my weight.

Adopting and Adapting to the 40-20-40 Macronutrient Ratio

Transitioning to a 40-20-40 ratio of fats, proteins, and carbohydrates might seem daunting, but it is about making incremental changes. Begin by analyzing your current eating habits and gradually adjust your intake. For example, if your diet is high in fats, start by introducing more whole-grain carbohydrates like quinoa and brown rice while scaling back on fatty meats and increasing lean protein sources.

The key is to maintain this ratio consistently. Choose meals and recipes that not only adhere to these macronutrient levels but also appeal to your taste preferences and lifestyle. Sustainability is about enjoyment and satisfaction just as much as it is about nutritional content.

Choosing the Right Foods

Selecting the right ingredients plays a crucial role in maintaining weight. Focus on foods that are nutrient-dense and minimally processed. Vegetables, fruits, whole grains, lean proteins, and healthy fats should make up the bulk of your diet. These foods are not only healthier but also more satiating, which can help prevent overeating.

Practical Tips for Daily Eating

- **Meal Planning:** Plan your meals ahead of time to avoid impulsive eating decisions that could lead to consuming foods that don't align with your macronutrient goals.

- **Cooking at Home:** Prepare most of your meals at home, where you have control over ingredients and cooking methods. Cooking at home can significantly reduce the intake of excessive calories and unhealthy ingredients found in many restaurant dishes.
- **Mindful Eating:** Be mindful of what and how much you're eating. Pay attention to hunger cues and stop eating when you're comfortably full. Avoid distractions while eating so you can truly enjoy your meals and recognize satiety cues more effectively

Exercise and Physical Activity

Maintaining weight isn't just about diet; regular physical activity is equally important. Exercise helps burn calories, but it boosts metabolism and enhances muscle mass, both of which are crucial for maintaining weight loss. Incorporate a mix of cardiovascular exercises, strength training, and flexibility routines into your weekly schedule.

Monitoring Your Progress

Keep track of your weight and body composition regularly but not obsessively. Occasional monitoring can help you notice trends and make necessary adjustments before significant weight regain occurs. Use tools like digital scales, body measurement tapes, and even wearable devices to keep an eye on your physical health.

Psychological Aspects

Maintaining weight loss is also a mental challenge. It involves changing the way you think about food and your body. Support from family, friends, or a community of like-minded individuals can provide motivation and encouragement. Consider joining online forums, local support groups, or even working with a counselor or therapist if you find it difficult to maintain weight on your own.

Long-term Sustainability

Ultimately, the key to maintaining weight loss is to view these changes not as temporary adjustments but as permanent improvements to your lifestyle. Make choices that you can sustain indefinitely, only once you've reached a certain number on the scale.

Conclusion

Weight maintenance is a continuous journey that doesn't end with the conclusion of a diet. It's an integral part of a healthy lifestyle. Remember, it's not about adhering to strict rules forever but about developing a balanced, enjoyable, and healthful eating pattern that you can maintain throughout your life. By embracing these principles, you ensure that your weight remains stable and your health is always protected. Embrace the challenge, enjoy the journey, and celebrate every moment of your health-focused life.

CHAPTER TWO
ACTION

Meal Prepping Made Easy

Following are my tops tips for making meal prep work for you!

Stock up on plenty of reusable glass or plastic containers and zip-top bags; they will become indispensable in simplifying your meal preparation. Consider containers with dividers to keep your meals well-organized.

Planning ahead helps minimize waste and maintain variety in your meals. Engage your family in the planning process to get everyone excited about the upcoming week's meals.

When you're new to meal prepping, start with a small, core collection of recipes

that your family enjoys. You'll soon know these recipes by heart!

Always make a shopping list before you go to the store, and make sure to stick to it.

Prepare food in large batches and store it in the fridge or freezer to use throughout the week. Keep ready-to-eat snacks like fruits, chopped vegetables, and nuts available for quick and easy snacking.

Dedicate a few hours each week to chopping and cooking. This upfront time investment will save you hours later.

Store berries and chopped vegetables in a large, divided container to make it easy for your family to grab a healthy snack on the go!

In a Nutshell:
 PLAN —> SHOP —> PREPARE

Meal Plans

Before embarking on my transformative five-week dietary journey, I meticulously prepared by crafting a daily macro measurement plan and a weekly grocery list.

This initial preparation was not just about organizing my meals but setting the stage for sustainable change. It ensured that every day was optimized for success, aligning my nutritional intake with my health goals.

This proactive approach allowed me to focus on progress rather than guesswork, making each meal a calculated step towards a healthier me. Let this be a testament to the power of preparation in achieving lasting health transformations.

Week 1

 MEALS & SNACKS

	MEAL 1	SNACK 1	MEAL 2	SNACK 2	MARCOS
MON	Egg Scramble	Kale Chips with Pecans	Grilled Chicken Salad	Asian Pear with Walnuts	Fat: 74% Protein: 18% Net Carbs: 8% Fiber: 29 g
TUE	Classic Smoothie	Kale Chips with Pecans	Burger with Grilled Eggplant	2 T chopped walnuts	Fat: 69% Protein: 19% Net Carbs: 12% Fiber: 35g
WED	Egg Scramble	½ cucumber with 2 T creamy dressing	Grilled Chicken Salad	1 oz 70%+ dark chocolate	Fat: 72% Protein: 17% Net Carbs: 11% Fiber: 26 g
THU	Classic Smoothie	Kale Chips with Pecans	Burger with Grilled Eggplant	½ cup raspberries	Fat: 67% Protein: 20% Net Carbs: 13% Fiber: 38 g
FRI	Grilled Chicken Salad	Cucumber Coconut Cashew Snack	Baked Salmon with Zucchini Medley	Coconut Chia Seed Pudding	Fat: 70% Protein: 23% Net Carbs: 7% Fiber: 25 g
SAT	Chef's Salad	Coconut Chia Seed Pudding	Baked Salmon with Zucchini Medley	½ cup raspberries 1 oz 70%+ dark chocolate	Fat: 73% Protein: 20% Net Carbs: 7% Fiber: 26 g
SUN	Classic Smoothie	Asian Pear with Walnuts	Chef's Salad	¼ cup pecans	Fat: 74% Protein: 18% Net Carbs: 9% Fiber: 32 g

Week 1 - Shopping List

Produce
- Raspberries
- Strawberries
- Lemons
- Asian pears
- Avocados
- Cucumbers
- Carrots
- Yellow Squash
- Zucchini
- Eggplant
- Tomatoes
- Lettuce
- Kale
- Spinach
- Onion
- Romaine or Butter Lettuce
- Garlic
- Thyme
- Parsley

Oils
- Olive Oil

Dairy
- Salted/Unsalted Butter
- Plain Greek Yogurt (full fat)

Protein
- Eggs
- Chicken
- Lean Ground Beef
- Salmon, Fresh
- Tuna, Canned

Misc. Spices
- Salt/Black Pepper/Sea Salt
- Paprika
- Cayenne
- Dried Oregano
- Pumpkin Pie Spice

Other
- Vanilla Extract
- Stevia/Monk Fruit
- Honey
- Black Olives
- Coconut Milk (full fat)
- Creamy Dressing
- Vinegar of Choice
- Unsweetened Coconut Flake
- 70%+ Dark Chocolate
- Pecans, Walnuts and Almonds
- Chia Seeds
- Cashew or Nut/Seed Butter of Choice

Week 3

 MEALS & SNACKS

	MEAL 1	SNACK 1	MEAL 2	SNACK 2	MARCOS
MON	Cheese and Veggie Omelet	1/4 cup walnuts with 1/4 cup raspberries	Baked Lemon Caper Wild Caught Salmon w/Asparagus and Cauliflower Rice	Chocolate Avocado Pudding	Fat: 70% Protein: 21% Net Carbs: 9% Fiber: 36 g
TUE	Baked Lemon Caper Wild Caught Salmon w/Asparagus and Cauliflower Rice	Chocolate Avocado Pudding	Rosemary Baked Chicken	1 medium cucumber 2 tbsp almond butter	Fat: 69% Protein: 23% Net Carbs: 8% Fiber: 34 g
WED	Rosemary Baked Chicken	Almond Chia Celery	Asian Beef Zoodles	Very Berry Bowl	Fat: 68% Protein: 23% Net Carbs: 8% Fiber: 33 g
THU	Asian Beef Zoodles	Very Berry Bowl	Rosemary Baked Chicken	1 oz 70%+ dark chocolate	Fat: 69% Protein: 21% Net Carbs: 10% Fiber: 27 g
FRI	Flaxseed Pancakes with Almond Butter and Blueberries	Aloha Avocado	Chicken Satay	1/2 oz 70%+ dark chocolate	Fat: 70% Protein: 20% Net Carbs: 10% Fiber: 27 g
SAT	Chicken Satay	Aloha Avocado	Flaxseed Pancakes with Almond Butter and Blueberries	1 medium cucumber 1 tsp Everything Bagel seasoning	Fat: 69% Protein: 21% Net Carbs: 10% Fiber: 28 g
SUN	Spicy Poached Eggs	Very Berry Bowl	Chicken Satay	Aloha Avocado	Fat: 72% Protein: 20% Net Carbs: 8% Fiber: 37 g

Week 3 - Shopping List

Produce
- Raspberries
- Strawberries
- Lemons
- Limes
- Avocados
- Asparagus
- Celery
- Broccoli
- Bell Peppe
- Spinach
- Onion and Chives
- Garlic
- Zucchini
- Rosemary

Dairy
- Cheddar
- Butter or Ghee
- Almond Milk
- Capers
- Baking Soda
- Vanilla Extract
- Unsweetened Cocoa Powder
- Liquid Stevia
- Unsweet Coconut Milk (full fat)
- Unsweet Coconut Flakes
- Salsa
- Wooden Skewers

Protein
- Eggs
- Chicken Breasts
- Lean Steak
- Salmon

Seasoning
- Salt and Black Pepper
- Pink Himalayan Salt
- Curry, Cayenne and Cinnamon
- Everything Bagel
- Tamari
- Liquid Aminos

Oils
- Olive Oil
- Coconut Oil

Nuts/Seeds
- Sesame Seeds
- Chia Seeds
- Ground Flax Seeds
- Walnuts
- Macadamia Nuts
- Almond Butter

Other
- Cauliflower Rice (frozen)
- Cauliflower Mash (frozen)
- Frozen Blueberries

Week 4

 MEALS & SNACKS

	MEAL 1	SNACK 1	MEAL 2	SNACK 2	MARCOS
MON	Olive Oil Coconut Oil	Chocolate Strawberry Almond Smoothie	Turkey Stuffed Peppers + Avocado Tossed Salad	Chocolate Pumpkin Energy Bites	Fat: 68% Protein: 22% Net Carbs: 10% Fiber: 36 g
TUE	Turkey Stuffed Peppers + Avocado Tossed Salad	1 small cucumber, 1 tsp lemon pepper or seasoning of choice	Pork Stir Fry, 1 cup riced cauliflower, 1 T toasted sesame seed oil	Chocolate Pumpkin Energy Bites	Fat: 70% Protein: 21% Net Carbs: 9% Fiber: 26 g
WED	Peanut Butter Mocha Smoothie	1 avocado with everything bagel seasoning	Pork Stir Fry, 1 cup riced cauliflower, 1 T toasted sesame seed oil	1/4 cup walnuts	Fat: 69% Protein: 18% Net Carbs: 12% Fiber: 37 g
THU	Peanut Butter Mocha Smoothie	Chocolate Pumpkin Energy Bites	Poached Herb Salmon, Roasted Asparagus + 2 T slivered almonds	Overnight Nut Salad	Fat: 69% Protein: 20% Net Carbs: 11% Fiber: 37 g
FRI	Poached Herb Salmon, Roasted Asparagus + 2 T slivered almonds	Overnight Nut Salad	Chicken Caesar Salad	1/2 cup strawberries 1/2 cup blueberries 2 tbsp heavy cream	Fat: 67% Protein: 24% Net Carbs:9 % Fiber: 26 g
SAT	Chicken Caesar Salad	1/2 cup strawberries 1/2 cup blueberries	Shrimp Scampi + 1 cup broccoli + 1 tbsp olive oil + 2 tbsp ground flaxseed	Mini Blackberry Parfait	Fat: 69% Protein: 20% Net Carbs: 11% Fiber: 35 g
SUN	Shrimp Scampi + Avocado Tossed Salad	1 small cucumber, 1 tsp lemon pepper or seasoning of choice	Taco Bowl	Mini Blackberry Parfait	Fat: 68% Protein: 20% Net Carbs: 12% Fiber: 43 g

Week 4 - Shopping List

Produce
- Strawberries
- Blackberries
- Lemons
- Limes
- Bananas
- Oranges
- Avocados
- Sprouts
- Cauliflower
- Cabbage
- Broccoli
- Lettuce of Choice
- Kale
- Jalapenos
- Cucumbers
- Asparagus
- Bell Peppers
- Zucchinis
- Mushrooms
- Herbs of Choice and Parsley
- Pico de Gallo
- Garlic
- Pumpkin Seeds
- Slivered Almonds
- Walnuts
- Unsweetened Peanut Butter
- Unsweetened Almond Butter

Dairy
- Butter
- Cream Cheese
- Sour Cream
- Plain Full Fat Greek Yogurt
- Cheddar/Monterey Jack
- Unsweetened Almond Milk

Protein
- Smoked Salmon
- Ground Turkey
- Pork Loin
- Chicken Breast
- Salmon
- Shrimp

Seasoning
- Salt/Pepper/Sea Salt
- Pink Himalayan Salt
- Red Pepper Flake
- Cinnamon or Pumpkin Pie Spice
- Stevia

Oils
- Olive Oil
- Coconut Oil
- Olive Oil Mayonnaise

Nuts/Seeds
- Chia Seeds
- Ground Flax Seeds
- Sesame Seeds
- Sunflower Seeds

Other
- Tamari
- Liquid Aminos
- Vanilla Extract
- Cocoa Powder
- Espresso
- Black Beans (canned)
- Black Olives (canned)
- Pumpkin Puree
- Protein Powder (low sugar/carb)

Week 5

 MEALS & SNACKS

	MEAL 1	SNACK 1	MEAL 2	SNACK 2	MARCOS
MON	Egg Avocado Boats	2 T hummus 10 baby carrots	Chicken in Peanut Sauce	Berries with Chia Cream	Fat: 68% Protein: 21% Net Carbs: 10% Fiber: 32 g
TUE	Chicken in Peanut Sauce	Blackberry Greek Yogurt Parfait + 1 T ground flax + 1 T chia	Shrimp Scampi	1 cup raspberries	Fat: 68% Protein: 23% Net Carbs: 9% Fiber: 29 g
WED	Shrimp Scampi	Citrus Avocado Salad	Pork and Green Bean Saute + 2 T ground flax seeds	Almond Chia Apple	Fat: 68% Protein: 20% Net Carbs: 12% Fiber: 29 g
THU	Pork and Green Bean Saute + 2 T ground flax seeds	Creamy Avocado Dip with Veggies	Lentil Stuffed Bell Pepper	Peanut Butter Cup Smoothie	Fat: 68% Protein: 20% Net Carbs: 12% Fiber: 33 g
FRI	Lentil Stuffed Bell Pepper	Strawberry Orange Smoothie	Lemon Thyme Halibut, Butternut Squash, Pumpkin Seeds and Brussels Sprouts	Creamy Avocado Dip with Veggies	Fat: 68% Protein: 18% Net Carbs: 14% Fiber: 38 g
SAT	Lemon Thyme Halibut, Butternut Squash, Pumpkin Seeds and Brussels Sprouts	Turkey Lettuce Wraps	Citrus Avocado Salad	Blackberry Greek Yogurt Parfait + 1 T ground flax, + 1 T chia	Fat: 71% Protein: 21% Net Carbs: 8% Fiber: 31 g
SUN	Scrambled Eggs with Spinach and Tomato	Chocolate Strawberry Almond Smoothie	Chicken Romaine Salad with Avocado	2 T hummus 10 baby carrots	Fat: 67% Protein: 23% Net Carbs: 10% Fiber: 29 g

Week 5 - Shopping List

Produce
- Strawberries
- Raspberries
- Blackberries
- Lemons
- Apples
- Oranges
- Grapefruit (optional)
- Avocados
- Chives
- Garlic
- Spinach or Kale
- Romaine/Lettuce of Choice
- Tomatoes
- Bell Peppers
- Zucchinis
- Green Beans
- Butternut Squash
- Brussels Sprouts
- Flat-Leaf Parsley
- Cilantro
- Ginger Root
- Pumpkin Seeds
- Sesame Seeds
- Sunflower Seeds
- Unsweetened Peanut Butter
- Unsweetened Almond Butter
- Pecans

Dairy
- Butter
- Parmesan Cheese
- Heavy Cream
- Bleu Cheese
- Greek Yogurt, Plain (full fat)
- Swiss Cheese
- Unsweetened Almond Milk

Protein
- Eggs
- Deli Ham and Turkey (nitrite/nitrate free)
- Pork Loin
- Chicken Breast & Rotisserie Chicken
- Halibut
- Shrimp

Seasoning
- Salt/Pepper/Sea Salt
- Red Pepper Flake
- Mrs. Dash Southwestern
- Cinnamon
- Thyme

Oils
- Olive Oil
- Coconut Oil
- Olive Oil Mayonnaise

Other
- Tamari
- Liquid Aminos
- Vanilla Extract
- Cocoa Powder
- Vinegar of Choice
- Unsweetened Coconut Flake
- Unsweetened Coconut Milk
- Cauliflower Rice (frozen)
- Lentils
- Protein Powder (low sugar/carb)

Nuts/Seeds
- Ground Flax Seeds
- Chia Seeds

Recipes

Cooking used to be a daunting task for me—entering the kitchen meant navigating a maze of pots, pans, and utensils, not to mention the array of spices and cooking oils. I was no chef, and frankly, I had little interest in the culinary arts. However, everything began to change when I started focusing on my health and exploring the Galveston Diet. My curiosity about how the ingredients in my recipes could impact my well-being transformed my approach to cooking.

I discovered that cooking isn't just about mixing ingredients; it's the art of nourishing your body and understanding what goes into it. As I delved into the recipes recommended by the Galveston Diet, I realized that each ingredient had a purpose, each measurement was significant, and every meal was an opportunity to enhance my health. This realization didn't turn me into a gourmet chef overnight, but it did ignite a passion for preparing meals that were beneficial for both my body and taste buds.

In this book, I share a collection of recipes that I've personally prepared and others that I've gathered from friends and family—all designed to promote good health and satisfy the palate. These recipes are more than just a list of ingredients and steps; they are a gateway to a healthier lifestyle. I've meticulously calculated the macros for each dish to help you integrate them seamlessly into your diet. Whether you're looking to maintain your current health regimen or make significant dietary changes, these recipes provide a practical framework for a nutritious diet.

For those who feel overwhelmed by the thought of cooking, I've structured each recipe to be straightforward and manageable. They require minimal kitchen equipment and use common ingredients that are both accessible and affordable. Moreover, each recipe includes tips on how to adjust flavors to your liking and substitutions for any dietary restrictions you might have.

Beyond the recipes, I emphasize the importance of understanding the nutritional content of your meals. This isn't just about counting calories but about knowing the balance of proteins, fats, and carbohydrates that your body needs. By following the guidelines I've laid out, you'll develop a keen sense of which foods serve your health goals best, transforming the act of cooking from a chore into a rewarding, health-boosting activity.

Ultimately, my journey from kitchen novice to health-conscious cook is a testament to the transformative power of diet and dedication. Through these recipes, I invite you to embark on your own culinary adventure. Not only will you learn to prepare delightful meals, but you'll also gain the knowledge to make informed choices about the foods you eat—choices that can dramatically improve your health and quality of life. Cook, eat, and thrive on the nourishment that comes from knowing you're feeding your body the best.

Avocado "Toast"

Ingredients:

- 8 hardboiled eggs, sliced
- 2 heads of cauliflower, cut into 1-inch slices
- 2 avocados
- Juice of 1 lemon
- Smoked paprika, to taste
- Salt, to taste
- Pepper, to taste
- Cooking spray (for the pan)

Instructions:

1. Prepare the Cauliflower:

- Heat a large pan over medium heat.
- Coat the pan lightly with cooking spray.
- Place the 1-inch slices of cauliflower in the pan. Cover the pan to allow the cauliflower to steam and cook more evenly.
- Cook each side of the cauliflower slices until they are nicely browned and tender, about 5-7 minutes per side.

2. Mash the Avocado:

- While the cauliflower is cooking, peel and pit the avocados.
- In a bowl, mash the avocados with a fork or potato masher until smooth.
- Add one lemon juice to the mashed avocados and mix well. This will enhance the flavor and help prevent the avocado from browning

3. Assemble the Avocado "Toast":

- Once the cauliflower slices are cooked, transfer them to serving plates.
- Spread a generous amount of the mashed avocado mixture on top of each cauliflower slice.
- Arrange the sliced hardboiled eggs on top of the mashed avocado.

4. Season and Serve:

- Season each assembled "toast" with smoked paprika, salt, and pepper to taste.
- Serve immediately while the cauliflower is still warm.

Macros (per serving):

- Net Carbs: 14g
- Fat: 21g
- Protein: 21g
- Serves 4 people

Preparation Time
20 minutes

Difficulty
easy

NOTE:

This Avocado "Toast" is a fantastic and healthful dish packed with nutrients and healthy fats, perfect for a quick and satisfying meal. Enjoy your culinary creation!

Egg Avocado Boats

Ingredients:

- **1 avocado** - Choose a ripe one for the best texture.
- **2 eggs** - You'll use these to fill the avocado halves.
- **1 slice lean ham, finely chopped** - Adds a savory, salty flavor.
- **Chopped fresh chives** - Optional, for garnish and a mild onion-like taste.
- **Salt and pepper** - To taste, for seasoning.

Instructions:

1. Prepare the Avocado:

- Preheat your oven to 350 degrees Fahrenheit (175 degrees Celsius).
- Slice the avocado in half and remove the pit. Using a spoon, scoop out a little extra avocado flesh where the pit was to create enough space for the egg. Be careful to maintain the integrity of the avocado shell.

2. Add the Eggs:

- Place the avocado halves in a small baking dish or a muffin tin to keep them stable.
- Crack an egg into a small bowl. Gently scoop out the yolk and some of the white, and carefully place it into one of the avocado halves. Repeat with the second egg and the other avocado half. Depending on the size of your avocados and eggs, you might not use all the whites to prevent overflowing.

3. Bake the Avocado Boats:

- Place the baking dish in the preheated oven and bake for about 20 minutes, or until the egg whites are set and the yolks are cooked to your desired firmness.

4. Add Toppings:

- While the avocados are baking, chop the slice of ham into small pieces.
- Once the avocados are done, remove them from the oven. Sprinkle the tops with salt and pepper.
- Add the chopped ham and, if using, sprinkle with chopped fresh chives for additional flavor and a pop of color.

5. Serve:

- Serve the egg avocado boats warm, ideal for a hearty breakfast or a nutritious snack.

Macros (per serving):

- Net Carbs: 2g
- Fat: 36g
- Protein: 19g
- Serves 2 person

Preparation Time
25 minutes

Difficulty
easy

Baked Eggs in Avocado

Ingredients:

- 2 eggs
- 1 avocado
- 1 tablespoon goat cheese, crumbled
- 1 slice of turkey bacon, chopped
- 1 tablespoon chives, finely chopped
- Salt, to taste
- Pepper, to taste

Instructions:

1. Preheat the Oven:

- Heat your oven to 425 degrees Fahrenheit (218 degrees Celsius).

2. Prepare the Avocado:

- Slice the avocado in half lengthwise and twist the halves to separate them.
- Remove the pit from each half. Using a spoon, scoop out about 1 to 1.5 tablespoons of avocado flesh from each half, creating a larger cavity. This will make space for the eggs.

3. Assemble:

- Place the avocado halves in a small baking dish or a muffin tin to keep them stable and upright.
- Carefully crack one egg into the cavity of each avocado half. It's okay if some of the egg white spills over.

4. Bake:

- Place the baking dish in the preheated oven and bake for 15-20 minutes, or until the eggs are cooked to your liking

5. Add Toppings:

- While the eggs and avocados are baking, cook the turkey bacon in a skillet until crispy, then chop into small pieces.
- Once the avocados are done baking, remove them from the oven.
- Sprinkle each half with salt and pepper.
- Add the crumbled goat cheese, chopped turkey bacon, and chives on top of the baked eggs.

6. Serve:

- Serve the baked eggs in avocado hot and enjoy immediately.

Macros (per serving):

- Net Carbs: 4g
- Fat: 36g
- Protein: 19g
- Serves 1 person

Preparation Time
25 minutes

Difficulty
easy

Scrambled Eggs with Spinach and Tomato

Ingredients:

- **8 eggs** - The base of the scramble, providing protein.
- **2 cups fresh spinach leaves** - Adds vitamins and a mild, earthy flavor.
- **1/2 cup chopped tomatoes** - Provides moisture and a bright taste.
- **1 tablespoon olive oil** - For cooking the eggs and adding a bit of healthy fat.
- **Salt and pepper** - To taste, for seasoning the eggs.
- **2 cups raspberries** - Fresh and sweet, serving as a refreshing side.

Instructions:

1. Prepare the Eggs:

- In a large mixing bowl, crack the eggs. Add a pinch of salt and pepper to taste.
- Whisk the eggs until they are well blended. This introduces air into the eggs, making them fluffier when cooked.

2. Cook the Eggs:

- Heat the olive oil in a large saucepan over low heat. It's important to use low heat to avoid burning the eggs and to ensure they cook gently, which improves their texture.
- Pour the egg mixture into the heated saucepan. Allow the eggs to cook undisturbed until a thin layer of cooked egg forms around the edge of the pan.

3. Add Vegetables:

- When the eggs start to set on the bottom, gently fold them with a spatula. This helps cook all parts evenly without overcooking.
- Halfway through the cooking process, add the fresh spinach and chopped tomatoes to the pan. The steam and heat from the eggs will help wilt the spinach and warm the tomatoes without losing their texture.
- Continue to push and fold the eggs, mixing in the spinach and tomatoes as you do. Keep cooking until the eggs are just barely set. They should still look slightly runny on top, which indicates they are perfectly soft and creamy.

4. Serve:

- Immediately remove the pan from heat to prevent the eggs from overcooking.
- Serve the scrambled eggs hot, with a small bowl of fresh raspberries on the side for a contrasting sweet touch.

Macros (per serving):

- Net Carbs: 8g (excluding the raspberries)
- Fat: 15g
- Protein: 12g
- Serves 4 person

Preparation Time
15 minutes

Difficulty
normal

Blackberry Greek Yogurt Parfait

Ingredients:

- 1/2 cup plain Greek yogurt
- 1/4 cup blackberries
- 1/4 cup pecans, roughly chopped
- 1 tablespoon chia seeds
- Cinnamon, to taste

Macros (per serving):

- Net Carbs: 15g
- Fat: 32g
- Protein: 23g
- Serves 1 person

Instructions:

1. Prepare the Ingredients:

- Wash the blackberries and set aside.
- Chop the pecans into smaller pieces if they are not already chopped

2. Assemble the Parfait:

- In a clear parfait cup or a small bowl, start by placing a layer of plain Greek yogurt at the bottom.
- Sprinkle a layer of chia seeds evenly over the yogurt.
- Add a layer of blackberries on top of the chia seeds.
- Add a layer of chopped pecans on top of the blackberries.

3. Top and Serve:

- Sprinkle cinnamon over the top of the parfait for added flavor.
- Serve immediately or chill in the refrigerator for a few minutes before serving if you prefer a colder dessert.

Preparation Time
10 minutes

Difficulty
easy

NOTE:

This Blackberry Greek Yogurt Parfait is perfect as a nutritious snack or even a light dessert. It's packed with protein from the Greek yogurt, healthy fats from the pecans, and antioxidants from the blackberries, making it a balanced and satisfying option. Enjoy your parfait!

Cheese and Veggie Omelette

Ingredients:

- 2 eggs
- 1 oz. shredded cheese (such as cheddar or your preferred type)
- 1/4 cup white onion, finely chopped
- 1/2 cup broccoli, finely chopped
- 1/2 cup spinach, roughly chopped
- 1/2 cup avocado, diced
- Olive oil or cooking spray (for greasing the pan)

Instructions:

1. Prepare the Vegetables:

- Wash and chop the broccoli, spinach, and onion. Dice the avocado.

2. Whisk the Eggs:

- In a medium bowl, crack the eggs and whisk them together until fully blended.
- Add the chopped onion, broccoli, spinach, and avocado to the eggs. Stir the mixture until everything is evenly distributed.

3. Cook the Omelette:

- Heat a non-stick skillet over medium heat and grease it lightly with olive oil or cooking spray.
- Pour the egg and vegetable mixture into the skillet. Spread the mixture evenly by tilting the pan slightly.
- Cook for about 2 minutes on a low flame, or until the edges start to lift from the pan.

4. Add Cheese and Finish Cooking:

- Carefully flip the omelette using a spatula.
- Sprinkle the shredded cheese over the top of the omelette.
- Cover the pan with a lid to allow the cheese to melt and the omelette to cook through, which should take another 2-3 minutes.

5. Serve:

- Once the cheese is melted and the omelette is fully cooked, slide it onto a plate.
- Serve hot.

Preparation Time
10 minutes

Difficulty
easy

Macros (per serving):

- Net Carbs: 6g
- Fat: 27g
- Protein: 24g
- Serves 1 person

Ingredients:

- 2 eggs - These will form the base of your scramble.
- **1 cup fresh spinach leaves** - Adds color, nutrients, and texture.
- **1/2 cup fresh tomatoes, chopped** - Provides a fresh, juicy flavor.
- **1 tablespoon butter** - For cooking the eggs and adding richness.
- **Salt and pepper** - To taste, for seasoning the eggs.
- **1 cup raspberries** - For a sweet, fresh side.

Egg Scramble

NOTES

This Egg Scramble recipe is a fantastic way to start your day, offering a balanced mix of protein, healthy fats, and antioxidants from the raspberries. It's quick to prepare, making it ideal for a nourishing breakfast or a quick brunch option.

Instructions:

1.Prepare the Egg Mixture:
- Crack the eggs into a mixing bowl.
- Add a pinch of salt and pepper to taste.
- Whisk the eggs until they are well blended and slightly frothy.

2. Cook the Scramble:
- Melt the butter in a large saucepan over low heat. It's important to keep the heat low to avoid burning the butter and to allow the eggs to cook gently, retaining a tender texture.
- Once the butter has melted and is slightly bubbling, pour the whisked egg mixture into the saucepan.
- Let the eggs cook undisturbed until a thin layer of cooked egg forms around the edge of the pan.

3. Add Vegetables:
- As the eggs begin to set around the edges, gently fold them towards the center with a spatula.
- Halfway through cooking, when the eggs are still slightly runny on top, add the fresh spinach and chopped tomatoes to the pan.
- Continue to gently push and fold the eggs around the pan, mixing in the spinach and tomatoes as you do. This technique helps to evenly cook the eggs while incorporating the vegetables.

4. Finish Cooking:
- Cook the eggs to your desired doneness. They should be barely set and slightly runny on top when you remove them from the heat. The residual heat will continue to cook the eggs on the plate.

5. Serve:
- Immediately transfer the scrambled eggs to a plate to prevent them from overcooking.
- Serve the scrambled eggs with a small bowl of fresh raspberries on the side.

Macros (per serving):

Preparation Time
15 minutes

Difficulty
easy

- Net Carbs: 8g (excluding the raspberries)
- Fat: 15g
- Protein: 12g
- Serves 1 person

Coffee Cocktail

Ingredients:

- 1 cup brewed coffee (hot or cold, depending on preference)
- 1 tablespoon MCT oil
- 1 scoop collagen powder
- 1/4 cup mixed nuts (such as almonds, walnuts, pecans, etc.)
- 1/4 cup blueberries
- Cinnamon, to taste

Instructions:

1.Prepare the Coffee:

- Brew 1 cup of coffee to your liking. This can be either hot coffee for a warm drink or chilled coffee if you prefer a cold beverage.

2. Mix MCT Oil and Collagen:

- Add 1 tablespoon of MCT oil and 1 scoop of collagen powder to the brewed coffee.
- Stir the mixture thoroughly until the MCT oil and collagen powder are completely dissolved. This step is crucial for ensuring the smooth texture of your drink.

3. Prepare the Snack:

- In a small bowl, combine the mixed nuts and blueberries.
- Dust with cinnamon to taste. This not only adds flavor but also boosts the antioxidant content of your snack.

4. Serve:

- Enjoy your Coffee Cocktail by sipping the coffee mixture.
- Eat the cinnamon-dusted nuts and blueberries on the side for a delightful and nutritious complement to your drink.

Macros (per serving):

- Net Carbs: 10g
- Fat: 34g
- Protein: 10g
- Serves 1 person

Preparation Time
5 minutes

Difficulty
easy

NOTE:

This Coffee Cocktail is perfect for an energizing snack, combining the stimulating effects of coffee with the nutritional benefits of MCT oil, collagen, nuts, and blueberries. Enjoy this wholesome and satisfying drink!

Smoked Salmon "Bagel"

Ingredients:

- 2 ounces smoked salmon
- 2 tablespoons cream cheese
- 1/2 cup sprouts (such as alfalfa or broccoli sprouts)
- 1 large slice of cauliflower (about 1-inch thick), cut vertically to form a "steak"
- Olive oil (for coating the cauliflower)
- Salt and pepper to taste (optional)

- Layer the sprouts over the cream cheese.
- Top with smoked salmon, arranging it neatly to cover the sprouts.

4. Serve:

- Serve immediately while the cauliflower is still warm or at room temperature.

Macros (per serving):

- Net Carbs: 5g
- Fat: 13g
- Protein: 15g
- Serves 1 person

Instructions:

1. Prepare the Cauliflower:

- Preheat your oven to 450 degrees Fahrenheit (232 degrees Celsius).
- Slice the cauliflower vertically into a 1-inch thick "steak." Depending on the size of your cauliflower, you might get 1-2 steaks per head.
- Lightly coat the cauliflower steak with olive oil. Season with salt and pepper if desired.
- Place the cauliflower on a baking sheet lined with parchment paper or lightly greased.

2. Bake the Cauliflower:

- Bake the cauliflower in the preheated oven for 10-15 minutes on one side.
- Flip the cauliflower steak carefully and continue to bake for another 10-15 minutes or until it's golden brown and tender.

3. Assemble the Smoked Salmon "Bagel":

- Once the cauliflower is baked, remove it from the oven and let it cool slightly.
- Spread the cream cheese evenly over the top of the cauliflower steak.

Preparation Time
20 minutes

Difficulty
normal

Almond Chicken with Broccoli

Ingredients:

- 1/2 cup almond butter
- Juice of 2 limes
- 2 1/2 tablespoons tamari (or soy sauce if not gluten-sensitive)
- 2 teaspoons minced garlic
- 2 cups full-fat coconut milk
- 1 teaspoon curry powder
- 1/2 teaspoon cayenne pepper (adjust according to heat preference)
- 1 pound chicken breasts or thighs, cut into 1-inch cubes
- 4 cups broccoli, cut into 1-inch pieces
- 1/4 cup ghee (or substitute with butter if unavailable)
- 1/4 cup sesame seeds, for garnish
- 1 bunch cilantro, chopped

Instructions:

1.Prepare the Marinade:

- In a medium bowl, combine almond butter, lime juice, tamari, minced garlic, coconut milk, curry powder, cayenne pepper, and half of the chopped cilantro. Stir until well mixed.

2. Marinate the Chicken:

- Add the cubed chicken to the marinade, ensuring each piece is well coated.
- Cover the bowl and refrigerate for at least one hour, or up to eight hours for deeper flavor.

3. Cook the Chicken:

- Remove the chicken from the refrigerator.
- Heat a pan over medium-high heat.
- Transfer the marinated chicken into the pan, discarding excess marinade.
- Stir fry the chicken for 7-10 minutes or until fully cooked and golden.

4. Cook the Broccoli:

- While the chicken is cooking, place another pan over medium-high heat.
- Add the broccoli and a few tablespoons of water to steam.
- Cover and cook for about 5-7 minutes, or until the broccoli is tender but still crisp.
- Drain any excess water, and stir in the ghee until the broccoli pieces are well coated.

5. Serve:

- Arrange the cooked chicken and broccoli on plates.
- Sprinkle the sesame seeds and the remaining chopped cilantro over the top of the dishes.

Macros (per serving):

- Net Carbs: 11g
- Fat: 68g
- Protein: 45g
- Serves 4 person

Preparation Time
30 minutes
(plus at least 1 hour
for marinating)

Difficulty
normal

NOTE:

This dish is the perfect balance of sweet and savory, and the almond butter marinade is full of flavor. Enjoy!

Broccoli and Cheese Chicken Bake

NOTE:

This Broccoli and Cheese Chicken Bake is perfect for a quick weeknight dinner that doesn't compromise on flavor. Enjoy this creamy, cheesy, and satisfying meal!

Ingredients:

- 1 pound cooked chicken breast, chopped or shredded
- 4 cups broccoli florets
- 2 tablespoons olive oil
- 1/2 cup sour cream
- 1/2 cup heavy cream
- 1 cup shredded cheddar cheese
- 1 teaspoon crushed garlic
- 1 teaspoon dried basil
- Salt, to taste
- Black pepper, to taste

Instructions:

1. Preheat the Oven:

- Preheat your oven to 375 degrees Fahrenheit (190 degrees Celsius).

2. Prepare Broccoli:

- Bring a large pot of water to a boil. Add the broccoli florets and boil for about 5 minutes, just until they are bright green and slightly tender.
- Drain the broccoli in a colander and set aside to cool slightly.

3. Prepare Chicken:

- If the chicken isn't already cooked and chopped, cook the chicken in a skillet with 2 tablespoons of olive oil over medium heat until fully cooked. Then chop or shred it.
- Place the cooked chicken in a large casserole dish.

4. Make the Sauce:

- In a separate bowl, combine the sour cream, heavy cream, crushed garlic, and dried basil. Season with salt and pepper to taste. Mix well to create a smooth sauce.

5. Assemble the Bake:

- Add the drained broccoli to the casserole dish with the chicken.
- Pour the cream sauce over the chicken and broccoli, stirring gently to ensure everything is evenly coated.

6. Add Cheese and Bake:

- Sprinkle the shredded cheddar cheese evenly over the top of the sauce-coated chicken and broccoli.
- Place the casserole dish in the preheated oven and bake for 7-10 minutes, or until the cheese is melted and bubbly.

Preparation Time
35 minutes

Difficulty
difficult

Macros (per serving):

- Net Carbs: 3g
- Fat: 26g
- Protein: 37g
- Serves 4 person

Buffalo Chicken Strips

Ingredients:

- 2 tablespoons ghee
- 2 cups raw kale, chopped
- 12 oz. chicken breast, sliced into 1/2 inch strips
- 1/2 cup buffalo sauce (choose a low-carb variety if necessary)
- Salt and pepper to taste
- 4 oz. blue cheese, crumbled

Macros (per serving):

- Net Carbs: 2g
- Fat: 22g
- Protein: 33g
- Serves 4 person

Preparation Time
20 minutes

Difficulty
hard

Instructions:

1.Cook the Kale:

- Heat the ghee in a large skillet over medium-high heat.
- Add the chopped kale to the skillet and sauté for 2-3 minutes, or until it begins to wilt and soften. Stir occasionally to ensure even cooking.

2. Add Chicken:

- Add the chicken strips to the skillet with the kale.
- Season with salt and pepper.
- Cook for 4-5 minutes, stirring occasionally, until the chicken is fully cooked and no longer pink in the center.

3. Serve:

- Remove the skillet from heat.
- Plate the chicken and kale.
- Sprinkle the crumbled blue cheese over the hot chicken and kale, allowing the cheese to melt slightly from the warmth of the cooked ingredients.
- Serve the buffalo sauce on the side for dipping.

NOTE:

A modern take on comfort food, these chicken strips make a healthy and satisfying meal. Serve at your next Super Bowl watch party and watch them disappear! Enjoy!

Chicken Alfredo with Crispy Bacon

Ingredients:

- 1 pound chicken breast, cut into 1-inch cubes
- 2 cups broccoli florets
- 1 cup spinach
- 4 slices bacon
- 2 tablespoons butter
- 1 cup heavy cream
- Salt and pepper to taste

4. Combine Ingredients:

- To the pan with the cooked chicken, gently add the spinach and the pre-cooked broccoli.
- Stir in the heavy cream and crumbled bacon.
- Season with salt and pepper to taste.
- Continue to cook for an additional 5 minutes, allowing the cream to heat through and the spinach to wilt.

5. Serve:

- Serve the Chicken Alfredo with Crispy Bacon warm, ensuring each plate is filled with a generous amount of chicken, vegetables, and sauce.

Instructions:

1. Prepare the Broccoli:

- Pour boiling water into a bowl and add the broccoli florets.
- Let them stand for about 10 minutes, or until they reach your desired tenderness.
- Drain the broccoli and set aside.

2. Cook the Chicken:

- In a large frying pan, melt the butter over medium heat.
- Add the cubed chicken to the pan and sauté for about 7 minutes, or until the chicken is fully cooked and golden brown. Stir occasionally to ensure even cooking.

3. Prepare the Bacon:

- While the chicken is cooking, place the bacon in another pan and cook over medium heat until crispy.
- Remove the bacon from the pan, let it cool slightly, and then crumble it into small pieces.

Preparation Time
20 minutes

Difficulty
normal

Macros (per serving):

- Net Carbs: 4g
- Fat: 40g
- Protein: 40g
- Serves 4 person

Chicken Salad Stuffed Avocado

Ingredients:

- **2 avocados** - pitted and partially scooped out to create a pocket
- **2 cups shredded rotisserie chicken** - Convenient and easy to use
- **1/4 cup red onion, finely chopped** - For a bit of sharpness and crunch
- **1/4 cup avocado oil mayonnaise** - For creaminess
- **1/4 cup plain full-fat Greek yogurt** - Adds tang and creaminess
- **2 teaspoons Dijon mustard** - For a touch of zest
- **Juice of 1 lemon** - To brighten the flavors
- **Salt and pepper** - To taste, for seasoning
- **Chopped parsley** - For garnish (optional)

- Net carbs: 6-8g
- Fat: High, as both avocado and mayo are fat-rich
- Protein: Moderate, thanks to the chicken and Greek yogurt
- Serves 4 person

Instructions:

1. Prepare the Avocados:
- Slice the avocados in half lengthwise and remove the pits. Use a spoon to scoop out some of the avocado flesh, creating a larger cavity in each half. Be careful not to break through the skin. Set the removed avocado aside in a small bowl.

2. Make the Chicken Salad:
- In a large mixing bowl, combine the shredded rotisserie chicken and finely chopped red onion.
- Add the avocado oil mayonnaise, full-fat Greek yogurt, and Dijon mustard to the bowl.
- Squeeze in the juice of one lemon. Mash the avocado you set aside and add it to the bowl.
- Fold all the ingredients together until well mixed. Season the mixture with salt and pepper to taste.

3. Assemble the Avocado Boats:
- Divide the chicken salad evenly among the avocado halves, spooning it into the cavities where the pits were.
- If desired, garnish each filled avocado half with chopped parsley for an extra touch of color and flavor.

4. Serve:
- Serve the avocado boats immediately to prevent the avocados from browning. They make a great light lunch or a healthy appetizer.

Chicken Alfredo with Crispy Bacon

Preparation Time
20 minutes

Difficulty
normal

Macros (per serving):

- Net Carbs: 2g
- Fat: 42g
- Protein: 34g
- Serves 1 person

Ingredients:

- 3 oz. cooked lean chicken breast, chopped or shredded
- 4 oz. Romaine lettuce, chopped
- 2 teaspoons olive oil
- 2 teaspoons mayonnaise
- 1 clove garlic, minced
- A dash of liquid aminos (or soy sauce as an alternative)
- Fresh lemon juice (from about half a lemon)
- 2 tablespoons sunflower seeds

Instructions:

1.Make the Dressing:

- In a small bowl, whisk together the olive oil, mayonnaise, minced garlic, liquid aminos, and lemon juice until well combined.
- Stir in the sunflower seeds.

2. Prepare the Salad:

- In a large bowl, combine the chopped Romaine lettuce with the cooked chicken breast.

3. Combine and Serve:

- Pour the dressing over the salad in the large bowl.
- Toss everything together to ensure the salad is evenly coated with the dressing.
- Serve immediately.

Chicken Caesar Salad

Ingredients:

For the Salad:

- **6 oz cooked lean chicken breast** - Rotisserie chicken is convenient and flavorful, but you can use any cooked chicken.
- **8 ounces Romaine lettuce** - Or any lettuce of your choice, washed and chopped.

For the Dressing:

- **4 teaspoons olive oil** - Forms the base of the dressing.
- 4 teaspoons olive oil mayonnaise - Adds creaminess to the dressing.
- **4 cloves garlic, minced** - Gives a strong, aromatic flavor.
- **Dash of liquid aminos** - A healthier alternative to soy sauce, adds umami flavor.
- **Lemon juice** - To taste, for freshness and acidity.
- **1/2 cup sunflower seeds** - Adds crunch and nuttiness to the salad.

Instructions:

1. Prepare the Dressing:
- In a small bowl, whisk together the olive oil, olive oil mayonnaise, minced garlic, a dash of liquid aminos, and enough lemon juice to suit your taste. This mixture should have a creamy yet pourable consistency.
- Add the sunflower seeds to the dressing, stirring to incorporate them fully. The seeds add a pleasant crunch and nuttiness that complements the other flavors in the dressing.

2. Assemble the Salad:
- In a large salad bowl, add the chopped Romaine lettuce.
- Cut the cooked chicken breast into bite-sized chunks or strips and add them to the bowl with the lettuce.

3. Toss the Salad:
- Pour the prepared dressing over the lettuce and chicken in the bowl.
- Toss everything together until the salad ingredients are evenly coated with the dressing. Ensure that the sunflower seeds are distributed throughout the salad for added texture in every bite.

4. Serve:
- Once well mixed, serve the salad immediately. This dish is best enjoyed fresh to maintain the crispness of the lettuce and the juiciness of the chicken.

Macros (per serving):

- Net Carbs: 5g
- Fat: High, due to the olive oil and mayonnaise.
- Protein: High, primarily from the chicken and sunflower seeds.
- Serves: 2 person

Preparation Time
10 minutes
(if using pre-cooked chicken)

Difficulty
normal

Chicken Cordon Bleu

Ingredients:

- 3 cups shredded cooked chicken (from about 2 lb chicken)
- 6 ounces ham, cut into bite-size pieces
- 4 ounces butter, melted
- 6 ounces cream cheese, softened
- 1 tablespoon Dijon mustard
- 1 tablespoon white wine (optional)
- 1 ounce lemon juice
- ½ teaspoon salt
- 6 ounces Swiss cheese, sliced

Instructions:

1.Preheat the Oven:

- Preheat your oven to 350 degrees Fahrenheit (175 degrees Celsius).

2. Layer Chicken and Ham:

- Lightly grease a 9x13 inch baking dish.
- Place the shredded cooked chicken evenly in the bottom of the dish.
- Layer the bite-sized pieces of ham over the chicken.

3. Prepare the Sauce:

- In a large bowl, use an electric mixer to combine the melted butter, softened cream cheese, white wine (if using), Dijon mustard, lemon juice, and salt.
- Blend until the mixture forms a thick, smooth sauce.

4. Assemble:

- Spread the sauce evenly over the chicken and ham in the baking dish.
- Lay the slices of Swiss cheese on top of the sauce.

5. Bake:

- Place the dish in the preheated oven and bake for 30-40 minutes, or until the dish is hot and the cheese is melted.
- If you desire a golden and bubbly top, switch the oven to broil for the last 2 minutes of cooking. Watch it closely to prevent burning.

Preparation Time
60 minutes
(including prep and cooking time)

Difficulty
normal

Macros (per serving):

- Net Carbs: 2g
- Fat: 37g
- Protein: 42g
- Serves 6 person

Chicken Romaine Salad with Avocado

Ingredients:

- 12 oz. chicken breast, grilled
- 5 cups Romaine lettuce, chopped
- 1 avocado, cut into 1/2 inch pieces
- 1/2 cup olive oil
- 1/2 cup mayonnaise

- 3 garlic cloves, minced
- 2 teaspoons liquid aminos (or soy sauce if unavailable)
- Juice of 1 lemon
- 1/3 cup sunflower seeds
- 10 cherry tomatoes

Instructions

1. Prepare the Chicken:

- Once your chicken breast is grilled, allow it to cool slightly if it is still hot.
- Cut the grilled chicken into 1/2 inch slices.

2. Assemble the Salad:

- In a large salad bowl, combine the chopped Romaine lettuce with the sliced chicken and avocado pieces.

3. Make the Dressing:

- In a small bowl, whisk together the olive oil, mayonnaise, minced garlic, liquid aminos, and lemon juice until well blended. This will create your salad dressing.

4. Combine and Serve:

- Pour the dressing over the salad in the large bowl.
- Toss everything together to ensure the salad is evenly coated with the dressing.
- Sprinkle the sunflower seeds over the top of the salad for added crunch.

Preparation Time
15 minutes

Difficulty
easy

Macros (per serving):

- Net Carbs: 3g
- Fat: 61g
- Protein: 29g
- Serves 4 person

Chicken Sautéed with Mushrooms

Ingredients:

- 8 chicken thighs, skin and bone on
- 2 cups sliced crimini mushrooms
- 1 tablespoon crushed garlic
- 1 small jar of capers, drained
- 1 small jar of green olives, sliced or whole
- 1/2 cup dry white wine

- 2 tablespoons olive oil
- Juice of two lemons
- Fresh basil, chopped (to taste)
- Salt, to taste
- Pepper, to taste
- Cajun seasoning, to taste
- 3 avocados, halved

Instructions

1. Preheat and Prep:

- Preheat your oven to 200 degrees Fahrenheit (93 degrees Celsius) to use for keeping the chicken warm later.

2. Brown the Chicken:

- Heat the olive oil in a large, heavy frying pan over medium heat.
- Add the crushed garlic and sauté briefly until fragrant.
- Place the chicken thighs skin-side down in the pan. Season with salt, pepper, and Cajun seasoning.
- Cook for about 5 minutes until the skin is browned and crisp.
- Flip the chicken thighs over and season again. Cook for another 5 minutes.

3. Add Flavorings and Simmer:

- Pour off the excess fat from the pan.
- Reduce the heat to low and add the sliced mushrooms, capers, and olives.
- Pour in the lemon juice and dry white wine.
- Cover the pan and let everything steam together for about 15 minutes, or until the chicken is fully cooked and tender.

4. Transfer to Oven:

- Transfer the frying pan to the preheated oven to keep the chicken warm until ready to serve.

5. Prepare Avocado and Serve:

- When ready to serve, plate each chicken thigh with a half avocado sprinkled with salt and pepper.
- Garnish the chicken with fresh basil.

Preparation Time
15 minutes

Difficulty
hard

Macros (per serving):

- Net Carbs: 4g
- Fat: 22g
- Protein: 28g
- Serves 6 person

Florentine Chicken Casserole

Preparation Time
25 minutes

Difficulty
normal

Ingredients:

- 3 cups chicken tenders, pounded thin or shredded Rotisserie chicken
- 2 tablespoons sun-dried tomatoes packed in oil
- 4 tablespoons warm water
- 12 fresh basil leaves
- 1/2 cup chopped yellow onions
- 1/4 cup chopped celery
- 8 oz. full fat cream cheese, softened
- 1 cup chicken stock
- 5 oz. baby spinach leaves
- 12 slices Provolone cheese
- 2 tablespoons olive oil
- Salt, to taste
- Garlic powder, to taste
- Pepper, to taste

7. Bake:

- Bake in the preheated oven for 15 minutes, or until the cheese on top is bubbly and lightly browned.

Macros (per serving):

- Net Carbs: 8g
- Fat: 45g
- Protein: 61g
- Serves 5 person

Instructions:

1. Preheat the Oven:

- Preheat your oven to 350 degrees Fahrenheit (175 degrees Celsius).

2. Prepare the Vegetables:

- Heat olive oil in a large saucepan over medium heat.
- Sauté the onions and celery until they are soft and translucent, about 5 minutes.
- Add the spinach to the pan and continue to sauté until it is wilted, about 2-3 minutes.

3. Cook the Chicken:

- Add the diced or shredded chicken to the saucepan. Sauté everything together for a couple of minutes just to combine the flavors. Season with salt, pepper, and garlic powder.

4. Make the Sun-Dried Tomato Purée:

- In a small blender or food processor, purée the sun-dried tomatoes along with 4 tablespoons of water until smooth.

5. Prepare the Cheese Mixture:

- In a medium mixing bowl, combine the sun-dried tomato purée, softened cream cheese, chicken stock, chopped basil, and additional salt, pepper, and garlic powder to taste. Mix until the mixture is smooth.

6. Combine and Assemble:

- Stir the sautéed chicken and spinach into the cheese mixture until everything is well combined.
- Spread the mixture evenly in a 9x13 inch casserole dish.
- Top with slices of Provolone cheese.

Grilled Chicken Breasts

Ingredients:

- 4 medium chicken breasts
- 1/2 cup olive oil
- Juice of 1 lemon
- 1/4 teaspoon salt
- 1/2 tablespoon black pepper
- 1 teaspoon garlic (fresh minced or garlic powder)

Preparation Time
20 minutes
(not including marinating time)

Difficulty
normal

Macros (per serving):

- Net Carbs: 0g
- Fat: 32g
- Protein: 37g
- Serves 4 person

NOTE:

I love to make grilled chicken when I can cook outside on the deck, but grilled chicken recipes can also be cooked on a stove top grill pan with ridges, or an electric griddle.

Instructions:

1. Prepare the Chicken:

- Take each chicken breast and cut slits in the top to allow them to cook evenly and absorb more marinade.

2. Make the Marinade:

- In a Ziplock bag, combine the olive oil, freshly squeezed lemon juice, salt, black pepper, and garlic.
- Place the chicken breasts in the bag with the marinade.
- Seal the bag and shake well to ensure the chicken is evenly coated with the marinade.

3. Marinate:

- Add the diced or shredded chicken to the saucepan. Sauté everything together for a couple of minutes just to combine the flavors. Season with salt, pepper, and garlic powder.

4. Grill the Chicken:

- Preheat your grill to medium-high heat.
- Remove the chicken from the marinade and place it on the grill.
- During grilling, brush the chicken with the excess marinade to keep it moist and add extra flavor.
- Grill the chicken for about 6-7 minutes on each side, or until the chicken is thoroughly cooked and the juices run clear.

Hot Chicken Salad Casserole

Ingredients:

- 2 cups cooked chicken, shredded (Rotisserie chicken recommended for convenience)
- 3/4 cup avocado mayonnaise
- 1 cup cooked brown rice
- 1 cup celery, diced
- 8 oz sour cream
- 1 tablespoon minced onion
- 1 tablespoon lemon juice
- 2 tablespoons butter
- 1 cup ground baked pork rinds

Macros (per serving):

- Net Carbs: 10g
- Fat: 39g
- Protein: 33g
- Serves 6 person

Preparation Time
60 minutes (including cooking time)

Difficulty
hard

Instructions:

1. Preheat the Oven:
- Preheat your oven to 350 degrees Fahrenheit (175 degrees Celsius).

2. Mix the Casserole Ingredients:
- In a large mixing bowl, combine the shredded chicken, avocado mayonnaise, cooked brown rice, diced celery, sour cream, minced onion, and lemon juice. Stir until all ingredients are well blended.

3. Prepare the Casserole Dish:
- Transfer the chicken mixture to a casserole dish, spreading it evenly.

4. Prepare the Topping:
- In a small saucepan, melt the butter.
- In a separate bowl, mix the melted butter with the ground baked pork rinds until the rinds are evenly coated.
- Sprinkle the pork rind mixture over the top of the chicken mixture in the casserole dish.

5. Bake the Casserole:
- Place the casserole in the preheated oven and bake for 30 minutes, or until the topping is golden and crispy and the casserole is heated through.

Grilled Chicken Salad

Ingredients:

- **grilled chicken** – All you have to do is make a simple marinade, let the chicken marinate for 1-12 hours and grill it up! The end result is chicken breasts that are juicy, tender and packed with flavor.
- **romaine lettuce** – the base of this salad! The romaine adds a nice crunch and pairs well with the rest of the ingredients.
- **cucumber** – adds a refreshing crunch.
- cherry tomatoes – these add a slightly sweet flavor and pop of color.
- **red onion** – adds a pungent and slightly spicy element.
- **grilled corn** – adds a slight sweetness and smokiness to the salad.
- **roasted sweet potatoes**

- **avocado** – adds creaminess and some healthy fats to this salad.
- **honey mustard dressing** – It's made with simple ingredients like dijon mustard, lemon juice, olive oil, apple cider vinegar and spices. Its sweet and tangy notes complement the flavors of the chicken and veggies brilliantly.

Macros (per serving):

- Net carbs: 3g
- Fat: 10g
- Protein: 27g
- Serves 1 person

Instructions

1. Marinate chicken:

- Start by whisking together vinegar, oil, garlic powder, thyme, oregano, salt and black pepper in a small bowl until well combined. Then, place the chicken in a shallow dish or a sealable plastic bag. Add the marinade to the chicken, toss to coat, and refrigerate for at least one hour or up to 12 hours.

2. Make dressing + prepare veggies:

- While the chicken is marinating, make your dressing and prep the remaining ingredients for the salad.

3. Grill chicken:

- Remove the chicken from the marinade, shaking off the excess and discarding the leftover marinade. Heat a grill or grill pan and once hot, place chicken breasts on the grill grates. Cook the chicken for about 5 minutes per side, or until it's cooked through and no longer pink. You want to check the internal temperature of the chicken with a meat thermometer to make sure it's at 165°F.

4. Assemble salad:

- To assemble the salad, start with a bed of romaine lettuce in two bowls. Top the lettuce with cucumber, tomatoes, onion, corn, roasted sweet potatoes, avocado and the sliced grilled chicken breast. Drizzle honey mustard dressing over the top and enjoy!

Preparation Time
30 minutes

Difficulty
easy

Italian Soup with Tomato and Zoodles

Ingredients:

- 1 pound Italian turkey or pork sausage
- 2 tablespoons olive oil
- 1 yellow onion, diced
- 4 cloves garlic, chopped
- 1/4 cup bell peppers, diced
- 1 zucchini, spiralized into noodles (zoodles)
- 1/2 cup tomatoes, diced
- 1 cup water
- Salt and pepper, to taste

Macros (per serving):

- Net Carbs: 11g
- Fat: 38g
- Protein: 24g
- Serves 4 person

Preparation Time
45 minutes

Difficulty
normal

Instructions:

1. **Cook the Sausage and Vegetables:**
- Heat the olive oil in a large saucepot over medium-high heat.
- Add the sausage, breaking it into smaller pieces as it cooks.
- Once the sausage starts to brown, add the diced onion, chopped garlic, and diced bell peppers.
- Sauté the mixture for about 10 minutes, or until the vegetables are softened and the sausage is thoroughly cooked.

2. **Add Tomatoes and Simmer:**
- Stir in the diced tomatoes and water.
- Season the soup with salt and pepper to taste.
- Bring the mixture to a boil, then reduce the heat to a simmer.
- Let the soup simmer uncovered for 20 minutes, allowing the flavors to meld together.

3. **Add Zoodles:**
- In the last 2 minutes of cooking, add the zoodles to the soup.
- Cook briefly to ensure the zoodles are just tender but still firm, preserving their texture.

4. **Serve:**
- Ladle the hot soup into bowls and serve immediately.

Beef Stuffed
Portobello Mushrooms

Ingredients:

- 4 large portobello mushroom caps
- 1/4 cup olive oil
- 8 oz. 90% lean ground beef
- 4 cloves of garlic, minced
- 1 cup cauliflower rice
- Salt and pepper, to taste
- 1/2 teaspoon dried oregano
- 1/2 teaspoon dried thyme
- 1/2 teaspoon dried basil
- 1/2 teaspoon dried rosemary
- 8 oz. parmesan cheese, shredded
- 2 cups fresh spinach

Macros (per serving):

- Net Carbs: 2g
- Fat: 37g
- Protein: 22g
- Serves 4 person

80

Instructions

1. Preheat the Oven:

- Preheat your oven to 400°F (200°C).

2. Prepare the Mushrooms:

- Place the portobello mushroom caps on a baking sheet.
- Bake in the preheated oven for 10 minutes.
- After baking, remove the mushrooms from the oven and use a paper towel to gently absorb any excess moisture from the caps. Set aside.

3. Make the Dressing:

- Heat the olive oil in a skillet over medium heat.
- Add the ground beef to the skillet, season with salt and pepper, and cook for 4-6 minutes, breaking the beef into smaller pieces as it cooks.
- Add the minced garlic and cauliflower rice to the skillet and continue to cook for another 4-6 minutes until the cauliflower rice begins to soften.
- Stir in the dried oregano, thyme, basil, and rosemary, mixing well to combine all the flavors.
- Add the fresh spinach to the skillet and cook until the spinach has wilted.

4. Stuff the Mushrooms:

- Spoon the ground beef and vegetable mixture into the prepared mushroom caps, distributing it evenly among them.
- Top each stuffed mushroom with shredded parmesan cheese.

5. Bake the Stuffed Mushrooms:

- Place the stuffed mushrooms back in the oven and bake for an additional 10 minutes, or until the stuffing is heated through and the cheese is golden and bubbly.

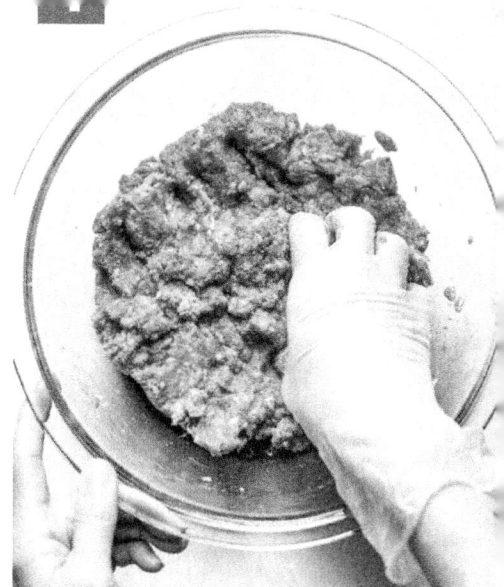

Preparation Time
30 minutes

Difficulty
hard

Burger with Grilled Eggplant

A great recipe when you are craving a burger. The grilled onions are an added bonus. You won't even miss the bun!

Ingredients:

- 6-8 leaves of green leaf or butter lettuce
- 2 tomatoes, sliced
- 1 avocado, sliced
- 1 yellow onion, sliced
- 1 pound lean ground beef, divided into 4 hamburger patties
- 2 medium Italian eggplants
- 1/4 cup olive oil, divided
- Salt and pepper to taste

- Wrap each burger with two or three overlapping lettuce leaves to hold everything together.

6. Serve:

- Serve each lettuce-wrapped burger with slices of grilled eggplant on the side.

Macros (per serving):

- Net Carbs: 16g
- Fat: 34g
- Protein: 28g
- Serves 4 person

Preparation Time
30 minutes

Difficulty
normal

Instructions:

1. Prepare the Eggplant:

- Slice the eggplant lengthwise into ⅓ inch slices.
- Brush both sides of each slice with olive oil and sprinkle with a little salt.

2. Cook the Onions:

- Heat 1 tablespoon of olive oil in a pan over medium-low heat.
- Add the sliced onion to the pan, season with salt and pepper, and sauté until the onions are golden brown and soft.
- Remove the onions from the pan and set aside.

3. Grill the Eggplant:

- Preheat a grill or grill pan over medium heat.
- Place the eggplant slices on the grill and cook for 3 minutes on each side, or until tender and grill marks appear.
- Tent the grilled eggplant with foil to keep warm.

4. Cook the Burgers:

- Return the pan used for the onions to medium-high heat and add another tablespoon of olive oil.
- Place the seasoned hamburger patties in the pan (or on the grill alongside the eggplant) and cook for 2-3 minutes on each side, or until the desired doneness is reached.

5. Assemble the Burgers:

- Top each cooked burger with the sautéed onions, tomato slices, and avocado slices.

Galveston Diet Meatloaf

This Is Easy To Make On A Sunday During Meal Prep And Divide Up Into Lunches; Or Prep And Shape Into Loaf And Chill To Serve On Monday Night (Throw It Into Oven When You Get Home!)

Ingredients:

- 1 ½ lbs ground beef (grass-fed and at least 90% lean)
- 1 cup almond flour
- 2 eggs
- ⅓ cup no sugar added tomato sauce
- ½ teaspoon salt
- ½ teaspoon black pepper
- ½ cup grated Parmesan cheese
- ¼ cup chopped onion
- ½ teaspoon garlic powder
- 2 tablespoons olive oil

Instructions:

1. Preheat the Oven:

- Preheat your oven to 350 degrees Fahrenheit (175 degrees Celsius).

2. Saute Onions:

- Heat olive oil in a skillet over medium heat.
- Add the chopped onions to the skillet and sauté until they become translucent and slightly golden, about 3-5 minutes.

3. Mix Ingredients:

- In a large mixing bowl, combine the ground beef, sautéed onions, almond flour, eggs, tomato sauce, salt, pepper, grated Parmesan cheese, and garlic powder.
- Mix all the ingredients together until well combined.

4. Shape the Loaf:

- Transfer the meat mixture to a shallow baking pan.
- Shape the mixture into a firm oval loaf. Make sure the loaf is evenly shaped to ensure even cooking.

5. Bake:

- Place the baking pan in the preheated oven and bake the meatloaf for 1 hour.
- The meatloaf is done when it is no longer pink in the center, and an instant-read thermometer inserted into the center reads 160 degrees Fahrenheit (71 degrees Celsius).

6. Serving:

- Remove the meatloaf from the oven and let it rest for a few minutes before slicing. This helps the juices redistribute throughout the meatloaf, making it moist and flavorful.
- Slice and serve warm.

Macros (per serving):

- Net Carbs: 4g
- Fat: 47g
- Protein: 61g
- Serves 4 person

Preparation Time
60 minutes

Difficulty
normal

Steak Salad with Herb Vinaigrette

Ingredients:

- 16 oz. top sirloin steak
- 1 tablespoon ghee or butter
- 4 cups fresh spinach leaves
- 12 cherry tomatoes, halved
- 1/2 cucumber, peeled and cut into bite-sized cubes
- 1 avocado, sliced
- 4 oz. blue cheese, crumbled
- 1/4 cup chopped pecans
- 1/4 cup red wine vinegar
- 1/2 cup olive oil
- Juice of 1/2 lemon
- 1/2 teaspoon dried oregano
- 1/2 teaspoon dried thyme
- Salt and pepper, to taste

Macros (per serving):

- Net Carbs: 5g
- Fat: 54g
- Protein: 43g
- Serves 4 person

Preparation Time
20 minutes

Difficulty
easy

Instructions:

1. Cook the Steak:

- **To Sauté:** Heat ghee or butter in a skillet over medium-high heat. Add the steak to the pan and cook for 3-4 minutes on each side for medium rare.
- **To Grill:** Preheat your grill. Grill the steak over high heat for 3-4 minutes on each side for medium rare.
- Once cooked, remove the steak from heat and let it rest for about 5 minutes.

2. Prepare the Vinaigrette:

- In a small bowl, whisk together the red wine vinegar, olive oil, lemon juice, dried oregano, dried thyme, salt, and pepper until well combined.

3. Assemble the Salad:

- In a large salad bowl, combine the spinach leaves, halved cherry tomatoes, cubed cucumber, and sliced avocado.
- Toss the salad with the herb vinaigrette until everything is lightly coated.

4. Add the Steak and Final Touches:

- Cut the rested steak crosswise into thin slices.
- Arrange the steak slices on top of the tossed salad.
- Sprinkle with the chopped pecans and the remaining blue cheese crumbles.

Zucchini Boat

Ingredients:

- 4 medium zucchini
- 2 cups ground beef or turkey (cooked)
- 1 can Rotel brand tomatoes (spicy or mild, based on preference)
- 1 cup mozzarella cheese, shredded
- Olive oil (enough for cooking, approximately 2 tablespoons)
- 1/4 cup walnut halves (for serving)

Instructions:

1. Preheat the Oven:

- Preheat your oven to 350 degrees Fahrenheit (175 degrees Celsius).

2. Prepare Zucchini:

- Heat olive oil in a non-stick saucepan over medium heat.
- Add the chopped onions and celery, and sauté until they are clear and slightly softened.
- Add the chicken tenders to the pan and continue to sauté until the chicken is fully cooked through.

3. Scoop Zucchini:

- In a small blender or food processor, combine the sun-dried tomatoes and warm water. Puree until smooth.
- Add the fresh basil leaves to the puree and process until the basil is finely chopped.

4. Cook Meat and Zucchini Flesh:

- In a medium mixing bowl, combine the sun-dried tomato basil puree, room-temperature cream cheese, garlic powder, salt, black pepper, and chicken stock. Mix until smooth and well combined.

Nutritional Information (per serving, 2 boats):

- Calories: 495
- Net Carbs: 9g
- Fiber: 4g
- Fat: 37g
- Protein: 29g

- Fold in the fresh spinach leaves and the cooked chicken mixture until everything is evenly

5. Assemble Zucchini Boats:

- Transfer the mixture into a 9x13 inch casserole dish, spreading it out evenly.
- Layer the provolone cheese slices over the top of the mixture.
- Place the casserole in the preheated oven and bake for 15 minutes, or until the cheese on top is bubbly and slightly golden

6. Add Cheese and Bake:

- Remove the casserole from the oven and let it cool for a few minutes before serving to allow the flavors to meld together.
- Serve warm.

7. Serve:

- Serve the zucchini boats warm, with walnut halves on the side for added crunch and nutrition.

Serving Suggestion:

To reheat, place the zucchini boats in the microwave or oven until heated through.

Preparation Time
60 minutes

Difficulty
normal

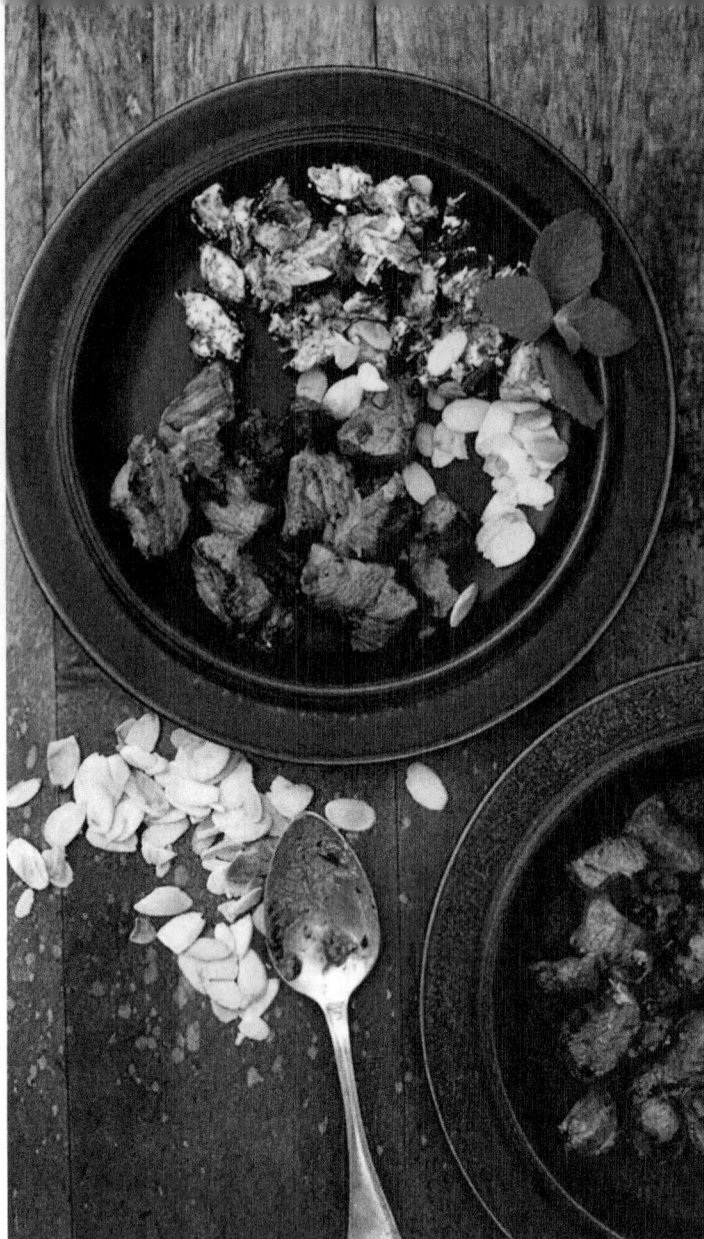

Ingredients:

For the Date-Yogurt Chutney:

- ¾ cup plain yogurt
- 1 teaspoon grated lemon zest
- 2½ teaspoons lemon juice
- 2 fat garlic cloves, finely chopped
- 5 tablespoons extra virgin olive oil
- 4 dates, pitted and finely chopped
- ¼ cup chopped cilantro

For the Lamb:

- 1 pound boneless leg of lamb, cut into 1-inch chunks
- 1 teaspoon kosher salt
- 1 teaspoon black pepper
- Extra virgin olive oil, for drizzling

For the Eggplant:

- 1 pound eggplant, cut into ¾-inch cubes
- 3 tablespoons extra virgin olive oil
- ¾ teaspoon kosher salt
- ¼ teaspoon black pepper

Charred Lamb and Eggplant With Date-Yogurt Chutney

NOTES

You can marinate the meat ahead of time or, in a pinch, make it while the eggplant roasts. Use half the marinade to slather the meat and to the rest, add almonds, dates and cilantro, and spread that over the finished cubes of eggplant. Then roast and broil the lamb to char the surface and keep the meat juicy and rare. Nice dinner!

Instructions

1. Marinate the Lamb:

- In a medium bowl, whisk together the yogurt, lemon zest, lemon juice, and chopped garlic. Gradually whisk in 5 tablespoons of olive oil.
- Season the lamb chunks with 1 teaspoon salt and 1 teaspoon pepper. Place the lamb in a large, nonreactive bowl, pour half of the yogurt mixture over it, and toss well. Cover with plastic wrap and refrigerate to marinate for at least 3 hours, or overnight.

2. Prepare the Eggplant:

- Preheat your oven to 425 degrees Fahrenheit (220 degrees Celsius).
- In a bowl, toss the cubed eggplant with 3 tablespoons of olive oil, ¾ teaspoon salt, and ¼ teaspoon pepper. Spread the eggplant on a baking sheet and roast in the oven, tossing occasionally, until it is golden brown and tender, about 20 to 30 minutes.
- Remove from the oven and scrape the roasted eggplant back into the bowl. Stir the chopped dates and cilantro into the remaining yogurt mixture, then toss with the warm eggplant.

3. Broil the Lamb:

- Adjust the oven setting to broil, and position a rack about 2 inches from the heat source.
- Remove the lamb from the marinade, wiping off any excess. Arrange the lamb on a large baking sheet and drizzle with a little olive oil.
- Broil the lamb until it is golden and cooked to your desired doneness, about 4 minutes for medium rare. Let the lamb rest for 5 minutes after removing it from the oven.

4. Toast the Almonds:

- While the lamb rests, heat a small skillet over medium-high heat. Add the sliced almonds and toast, tossing occasionally, until golden brown, about 3 minutes.

5. Serve:

- Divide the charred lamb among serving plates. Spoon the date-yogurt chutney with eggplant next to the lamb. Garnish each plate with toasted almonds and fresh mint.

Macros (per serving):

- Net Carbs: 32g
- Fat: 83g
- Protein: 33g
- Serves 4 person

Preparation Time

Approximately 3 hours for marinating (can be done overnight) + 25 minutes cooking time.

Difficulty

easy

Lamb Chop with Zucchini & Mint

Ingredients:

- **1 pound lamb chops** - This typically includes 4 chops depending on their size.
- **3-4 zucchini and/or summer squash** - Depending on size, these should be sliced or chopped.
- **3-4 tablespoons olive oil** - Used for sautéing the vegetables.
- **Fresh mint leaves** - For garnishing the lamb chops.
- **Salt and pepper** - For seasoning the lamb chops.

4. Garnish and Serve:

- Once the lamb chops are cooked to your desired level of doneness, remove them from the oven and let them rest for a few minutes.
- Serve the lamb chops with a side of the sautéed zucchini/squash.
- Garnish each lamb chop with fresh mint leaves for a refreshing contrast to the rich meat.

Macros (per serving):

- Net Carbs: 3g
- Fat: 37g
- Protein: 27g
- Serves 4 person

Instructions:

1. Preheat the Oven:

- Preheat your oven to 300 degrees Fahrenheit (150 degrees Celsius). This low and slow cooking method will ensure the lamb chops are tender and cooked evenly.

2. Season and Cook the Lamb Chops:

- Season the lamb chops generously with salt and pepper on both sides.
- Place the lamb chops in a baking dish or on a rack in an oven-safe pan.
- Cook in the preheated oven for about 30 minutes per pound. For 1 pound of lamb chops, this usually means around 30 minutes total, but adjust the time based on the thickness and your preference for doneness.

3. Sauté the Zucchini/Squash:

- While the lamb is cooking, slice or chop the zucchini and/or summer squash.
- Heat the olive oil in a large skillet over medium heat.
- Add the sliced or chopped zucchini/squash to the skillet. Season with salt, pepper, and any desired dried herbs (such as oregano, thyme, or basil) to enhance the flavor.
- Sauté until the vegetables are tender and lightly browned, about 8-10 minutes, stirring occasionally.

MOUSSAKA

Our classic Greek moussaka recipe epitomises the richness and comforting nature of hearty Greek fare. For me, this recipe brings back memories of childhood dinners (the kind everyone at our table would gladly eat!).

LISA G.A

- Net Carbs: 11g
- Fat: 48g
- Protein: 35g
- Serves 4 person

Preparation Time
02 hours

Difficulty
normal

Ingredients:

- 2 large eggplants, thinly sliced
- Olive oil cooking spray
- 1 tablespoon olive oil
- 1 medium brown onion, finely chopped
- 2 garlic cloves, crushed
- 800g lamb mince
- 400g can diced tomatoes
- 1 teaspoon ground cinnamon
- 1/3 cup pizza blend shredded cheese
- 1/2 teaspoon ground allspice
- Lemon wedges, to serve

For the White Sauce:

- 75g butter
- 1/3 cup plain flour
- 2 cups milk

1. Prepare the Eggplant:

- Spray the eggplant slices with olive oil cooking spray.
- Heat a large frying pan over medium-high heat. Cook the eggplant slices in batches for 2 to 3 minutes on each side or until browned. Transfer to a large plate and set aside.

2. Make the Lamb Mince Sauce:

- Heat 1 tablespoon of olive oil in a large saucepan over medium-high heat. Add the finely chopped onion and crushed garlic. Cook, stirring, for about 5 minutes or until the onion has softened.
- Add the lamb mince to the pan. Break up the mince with a wooden spoon and cook for 6 to 8 minutes or until the mince is fully browned.
- Stir in the diced tomatoes, ground cinnamon, and ground allspice. Bring the mixture to a boil, then reduce heat to medium-low. Simmer for 30 minutes or until the sauce is thick and most of the liquid has evaporated.

3. Prepare the White Sauce:

- In a separate saucepan, melt the butter over medium-high heat. Add the flour and cook, stirring, for 1 minute until bubbling.
- Gradually add the milk, stirring continuously to prevent lumps. Bring the mixture to a boil, then reduce the heat to medium. Continue cooking and stirring for 5 minutes or until the sauce thickens. Remove from heat.

4. Assemble the Moussaka:

- Preheat the oven to 180°C (160°C fan-forced). Grease an 8 cup-capacity ovenproof dish.
- Layer one-third of the eggplant slices, slightly overlapping, at the bottom of the dish. Spread half of the lamb mince sauce over the eggplant. Repeat with another layer of eggplant and the remaining mince sauce. Finish with a final layer of eggplant.
- Pour the white sauce over the top layer of eggplant. Sprinkle with shredded cheese.

5. Bake the Moussaka:

- Bake in the preheated oven for 45 minutes, or until the top is golden brown and bubbly.
- Let the moussaka stand for 15 minutes before serving. This helps the layers set and makes it easier to serve.

6. Serve:

- Cut into portions and serve hot with lemon wedges on the side for squeezing over.

Blueberry & Spinach Collagen Smoothie

Ingredients:

- 1 tablespoon chia seeds
- 1/2 cup water, divided
- 1 tablespoon coconut oil
- 1 tablespoon almond butter
- 1 tablespoon coconut flakes
- 1 tablespoon grated ginger
- 1 cup spinach (raw or frozen)
- 1 cup blueberries (raw or frozen)
- 2 scoops flavorless collagen
- 1/4 tablespoon cinnamon
- Dash of salt
- 4-6 ice cubes

Macros (per serving):

- Net Carbs: 19g
- Fat: 32g
- Protein: 19g
- Serves 1 person

Preparation Time
15 minutes

Difficulty
easy

Instructions:

1. Soak the Chia Seeds:

- Soak 1 tablespoon of chia seeds in 1/4 cup of water for 10-15 minutes. This helps them to expand and become gel-like, which will add a nice texture to your smoothie.

2. Prepare the Smoothie Base:

- In a blender, add the remaining 1/4 cup of water, 1 tablespoon of coconut oil, 1 tablespoon of almond butter, 1 tablespoon of grated ginger, 1 cup of spinach, 1 cup of blueberries, 2 scoops of flavorless collagen, 1/4 tablespoon of cinnamon, and a dash of salt.

3. Blend with Ice and Chia:

- After the chia seeds have soaked, add them to the blender along with 4-6 ice cubes. Blend all the ingredients together until smooth.

4. Adjust Consistency:

- If the smoothie is too thick, you can add a bit more water or nut milk to reach your desired consistency.

5. Serve Immediately:

- Pour the smoothie into a glass and enjoy immediately for the best flavor and texture.

Blueberry Pie Smoothie

Ingredients:

- 2 scoops collagen powder - Provides protein and supports skin, hair, and nail health.
- 1/2 cup water or unsweetened nut milk - Use more as needed to adjust consistency.
- 1 scoop MCT powder -
- 1 cup spinach -
- 1/2 cup blueberries -
- 2 tablespoons chia seeds
- 2 tablespoons flaxseeds
- 2 tablespoons almond butter
- Dash of almond extract
- Nutmeg

Instructions:

1. Blend Ingredients:

- Place all ingredients into a blender: 2 scoops of collagen powder, 1/2 cup of water or unsweetened nut milk (add more if needed later for desired consistency), 1 scoop of MCT powder, 1 cup of spinach, 1/2 cup of blueberries, 2 tablespoons each of chia seeds, flaxseeds, and almond butter, a dash of almond extract, and a sprinkle of nutmeg.

2. Adjust Consistency:

- Blend all the ingredients until smooth. After blending, check the consistency. If the smoothie is too thick, gradually add more water or unsweetened nut milk until you reach the perfect smoothness.

Macros (per serving):

- Net Carbs: 12g
- Fat: 37g
- Protein: 17g
- Serves 1 person

Preparation Time
10 minutes

Difficulty
easy

Blueberry Yogurt Smoothie

Ingredients:

- 2 ounces plain Greek yogur
- 1/2 cup kale
- 1/2 cup blueberries
- 2 tablespoons almond butter
- 1 tablespoon chia seeds
- Water or unsweetened nut milk (as needed)

Macros (per serving):

- Net Carbs: 15g
- Fat: 24g
- Protein: 14g
- Serves 1 person

Instructions:

1. Blend the Ingredients:

- Place 2 ounces of plain Greek yogurt, 1/2 cup of kale (washed and stems removed), 1/2 cup of blueberries, 2 tablespoons of almond butter, and 1 tablespoon of chia seeds into a blender.

2. Adjust Consistency:

- Blend until all the ingredients are thoroughly combined and smooth. If the smoothie is too thick, gradually add water or unsweetened nut milk until you achieve your desired consistency.

Preparation Time
05 minutes

Difficulty
easy

Chocolate Orange Smoothie

Ingredients:

- 1 cup canned unsweetened coconut milk
- 2 tablespoons cacao powder
- 1/2 fresh orange, peeled and sliced
- 1 tablespoon MCT oil
- 1 scoop low carb protein powder

Macros (per serving):

- Net Carbs: 17g
- Fat: 62g
- Protein: 13g
- Serves 1 person

Preparation Time
30 minutes

Difficulty
easy

Instructions:

1. Combine Ingredients:

- Place 1 cup of unsweetened coconut milk, 2 tablespoons of cacao powder, the slices of 1/2 a fresh orange, 1 tablespoon of MCT oil, and 1 scoop of low carb protein powder into a blender.

2. Blend Until Smooth:

- Blend all the ingredients together until the mixture is smooth and creamy. The orange should be completely integrated with no large pieces remaining.

3. Adjust Consistency:

- If the smoothie is too thick or too rich, gradually add water or additional unsweetened nut milk to thin it to your preferred consistency.

Chocolate Strawberry Smoothie

Ingredients:

- 1 scoop protein powder
- 1 cup kale
- 1/2 cup strawberries
- 1 tablespoon flax seeds
- 1 tablespoon almond butter
- 1 tablespoon cacao powder
- 1/2 cup coconut milk
- Ice

Macros (per serving):

- Net Carbs: 16g
- Fat: 38g
- Protein: 31g
- Serves 1 person

Preparation Time
05 minutes

Difficulty
easy

Instructions:

1. Blend the Ingredients:

- Place 1 scoop of protein powder, 1 cup of kale, 1/2 cup of strawberries, 1 tablespoon of flax seeds, 1 tablespoon of almond butter, 1 tablespoon of cacao powder, 1/2 cup of coconut milk, and a handful of ice into a blender.

2. Achieve Smooth Consistency:

- Blend all ingredients until smooth. If the smoothie is too thick or if you prefer a lighter consistency, add a bit of water or unsweetened nut milk gradually until it reaches your desired thickness.

Deluxe Smoothie Bowl

Ingredients:

- 1 cup frozen berries of choice
- 1 frozen banana
- 1/4 cup plain Greek yogurt
- 2 tablespoons almond butter
- 3/4 cup unsweetened coconut milk
- 1 tablespoon granola
- 1/4 cup fresh berries
- 1 tablespoon unsweetened coconut flakes
- 1/2 tablespoon chia seeds
- 1 tablespoon almonds
- 1 tablespoon pecans

Instructions:

1. Blend the Base:

- In a blender, combine 1 cup of frozen berries, 1 frozen banana, 1/4 cup of plain Greek yogurt, 2 tablespoons of almond butter, and 3/4 cup of unsweetened coconut milk. Add a few ice cubes for extra chilliness. Blend until the mixture is smooth and creamy.

2. Assemble the Bowl:

- Pour the smoothie mixture into a bowl. Evenly distribute 1 tablespoon of granola, 1/4 cup of fresh berries, 1 tablespoon of unsweetened coconut flakes, 1/2 tablespoon of chia seeds, 1 tablespoon of almonds, and 1 tablespoon of pecans over the top as toppings.

Macros (per serving):

- Net Carbs: 47g
- Fat: 53g
- Protein: 24g
- Serves 1 person

Preparation Time
15 minutes

Difficulty
easy

Greek Yogurt Parfait or Smoothie

Ingredients:

- 3/4 cup plain Greek yogurt
- 3 tablespoons chia seeds
- 1/4 cup almonds (use almond butter if making a smoothie)
- 1/2 cup strawberries or blueberries
- Water or unsweetened milk (as needed for the smoothie)

Macros (per serving):

- Net Carbs: 15g
- Fat: 20g
- Protein: 23g
- Serves 1 person

Instructions:

1. Blend Ingredients:

- Place the Greek yogurt, 3 tablespoons of chia seeds, 1/4 cup of almond butter (instead of whole almonds), and 1/2 cup of strawberries or blueberries into a blender.
- Start blending, gradually adding water or unsweetened milk to achieve your desired consistency until the mixture is smooth.

2. Prepare Ingredients:

- If using strawberries, cut them into halves or quarters depending on their size. Roughly chop the 1/4 cup of almonds.

3. Assemble the Parfait:

- In a bowl, layer 3/4 cup of plain Greek yogurt, followed by the prepared berries and almonds on top.
- Sprinkle 3 tablespoons of chia seeds over the berries and nuts.

Preparation Time
10 minutes

Difficulty
easy

Green Almond Butter Smoothie

Ingredients:

- 1/2 scoop low carb protein powder
- 1 tablespoon almond butter
- 1 cup kale
- 1/4 cup berries (choose your preferred type, such as blueberries or mixed berries)
- Ice

Macros (per serving):

- Net Carbs: 7g
- Fat: 10g
- Protein: 17g
- Serves 1 person

Instructions:

1. Blend Ingredients:

- Place 1/2 scoop of low carb protein powder, 1 tablespoon of almond butter, 1 cup of kale, 1/4 cup of berries, and a handful of ice into a blender.

2. Adjust Consistency:

- Blend all the ingredients until smooth. If the smoothie is too thick or if you prefer a thinner consistency, gradually add water or unsweetened nut milk until it reaches your desired thickness.

Preparation Time
05 minutes

Difficulty
easy

Raspberry Almond Smoothie

Ingredients:

- 3/4 cup plain Greek yogurt
- 3 tablespoons chia seeds
- 1/4 cup almonds
- 1/2 cup raspberries (or strawberries, depending on availability)

Instructions:

1. Prepare the Raspberries:
- Wash the raspberries thoroughly and gently pat them dry to remove excess water.

2. Blend the Ingredients:
- Place the 3/4 cup of plain Greek yogurt, 3 tablespoons of chia seeds, 1/4 cup of almonds, and 1/2 cup of raspberries into a blender.

3. Adjust Consistency:
Blend until the mixture is smooth. If the smoothie is too thick, gradually add water or unsweetened nut milk to achieve your desired consistency.

Macros (per serving):

- Net Carbs: 17g
- Fat: 44g
- Protein: 19g
- Serves 1 person

Preparation Time
05 minutes

Difficulty
easy

Peanut Butter Cup Smoothie

Ingredients:

- 2 oz. plain Greek yogurt
- 2 tablespoons unsweetened cacao powder
- 2 tablespoons natural peanut butter
- 1 tablespoon flaxseed
- Dash of vanilla extract
- Ice

Instructions:

1. Blend the Ingredients:

- In a blender, combine 2 oz. of plain Greek yogurt, 2 tablespoons of unsweetened cacao powder, 2 tablespoons of natural peanut butter, 1 tablespoon of flaxseed, a dash of vanilla extract, and a handful of ice.

2. Adjust Consistency:

- Blend until the mixture is smooth. If the smoothie is too thick or if you prefer a thinner consistency, gradually add water or unsweetened nut milk until it reaches your desired thickness.

Macros (per serving):

- Net Carbs: 9g
- Fat: 18g
- Protein: 16g
- Serves 1 person

Preparation Time
05 minutes

Difficulty
easy

Broiled Tomato Bites

Ingredients:

- 1 pound Campari tomatoes, halved
- Extra-virgin olive oil, for drizzling
- Honey, for drizzling
- Aleppo-style pepper or Urfa biber, for sprinkling
- Flaky sea salt and freshly ground black pepper
- Parmesan cheese, grated (quantity based on preference)

Macros (per serving):

- Net Carbs: 8g
- Fat: 15g
- Protein: 4g
- Serves 1 person

Preparation Time
10 minutes

Difficulty
easy

Instructions:

1. Prepare the Oven:
- Preheat the broiler of your oven on high.

2. Prepare Tomatoes:
- Cut the tomatoes in halves.
- Cut a small sliver off the bottom of each tomato half so they can stand upright on a baking dish.

3. Arrange Tomatoes:
- Spray a baking dish with cooking spray or lightly grease it with oil.
- Place all the tomato halves, cut side up, on the dish.

4. Season:
- Drizzle olive oil over the tomato halves.
- Optionally, drizzle a small amount of honey on each tomato for added sweetness.
- Sprinkle with grated Parmesan cheese, covering the top of each tomato.

5. Broil:
- Place the baking dish in the oven under the broiler.
- Broil for about 3 minutes, or until the Parmesan cheese is golden and bubbly.

6. Finish and Serve:
- Remove the tomatoes from the oven.
- Sprinkle Aleppo-style pepper or Urfa biber, flaky sea salt, and freshly ground black pepper over the tomatoes.
- Serve hot as an appetizer or a side dish.

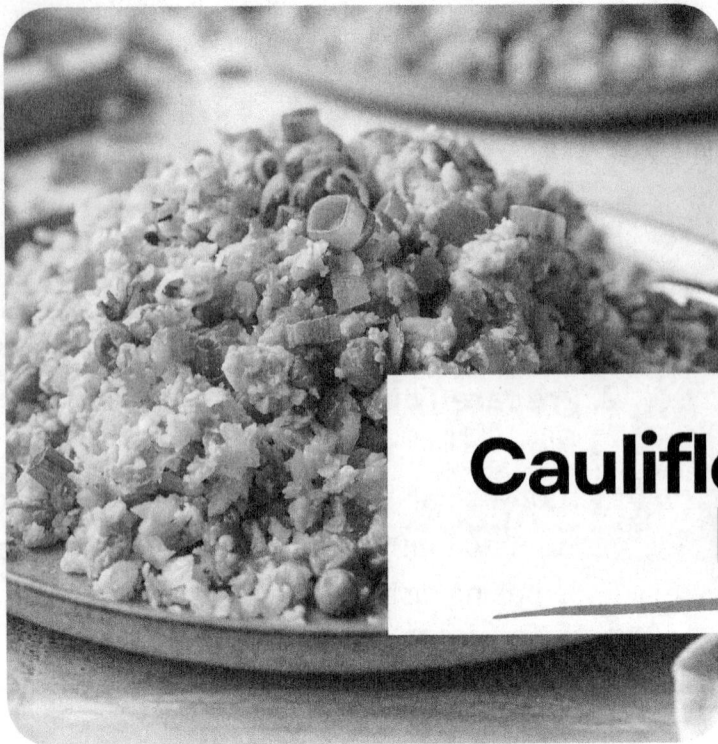

Cauliflower Fried Rice

Ingredients:

- 2 tablespoons vegetable oil
- 1 onion, peeled and diced
- 1 red bell pepper, deseeded and finely chopped
- 115 g (2/3 cup) frozen peas
- 1 clove garlic, peeled and minced
- ½ tablespoon sesame oil
- 300 g (10.5 oz) cauliflower, about 1 large head, grated/riced (approximately 3 cups once riced)
- 2 eggs
- 2 tablespoons dark soy sauce
- ¼ teaspoon salt
- 1 teaspoon lemon juice
- Optional: ½ bunch of spring onions (scallions), chopped for garnish

Instructions:

1. Prepare Cauliflower:
- Grate the cauliflower using a box grater or pulse in a food processor until it resembles rice.

2. Cook Onion:
- Heat the vegetable oil in a large wok or skillet over medium heat.
- Add the diced onion and cook, stirring regularly, for about 5 minutes until the onion becomes soft and translucent.

3. Add Vegetables:
- Add the chopped red bell pepper, minced garlic, and frozen peas to the wok.
- Cook for an additional 2 minutes, stirring regularly.

4. Cook Cauliflower:
- Stir in the sesame oil and then add the riced cauliflower.

- Increase the heat to high and cook, tossing frequently with a spatula to prevent sticking, until the cauliflower is heated through, about 3-4 minutes.

5. Add Eggs:
- Push the cauliflower mixture to one side of the wok.
- Crack the eggs into the cleared space and add a splash of soy sauce to the eggs.
- Allow the eggs to set slightly, then scramble until mostly cooked but still slightly runny.

6. Combine and Season:
- Mix the scrambled eggs into the cauliflower rice.
- Pour in the remaining soy sauce and sprinkle the salt over the mixture.
- Stir everything together to distribute the seasonings evenly.

7. Finish with Lemon Juice:
- Add the lemon juice, stir well, and taste. Adjust with more lemon juice if desired.

8. Serve:
- Divide the cauliflower fried rice between two bowls.
- Garnish with chopped spring onions if using.

Macros (per serving):
- Net carbs: 7g
- Fat: 13g
- Protein: 10g
- Serves 4 person

Preparation Time
30 minutes

Difficulty
easy

Cheesy Bacon Butternut Squash

No matter what the centerpiece of your meal is, this cheesy squash skillet is sure to steal the show. The balance of sweet, salty, and creamy is EXTREMELY addictive.

Ingredients:

- **2 butternut squash** - Cut in half lengthwise and seeded.
- **1 package of bacon, chopped** - This will add a rich, savory flavor.
- **1 yellow onion, diced** - Adds sweetness and texture.
- **3 cloves garlic, chopped** - For a hint of sharp, aromatic flavor.
- **1 cup spinach, chopped** - Adds color and nutrients.
- **2 cups mixed shredded cheese** - Use a blend of your favorite cheeses for melting.
- **Salt and pepper** - To taste, for seasoning the filling.

Instructions:

1. Prepare the Squash:

- Preheat your oven to 350 degrees Fahrenheit (175 degrees Celsius).
- Cut the butternut squash in half lengthwise and scoop out all the seeds.
- Place the squash halves cut side down in an oven-safe pan. Add about 1 inch of water to the pan; this helps the squash cook evenly and stay moist.
- Bake in the preheated oven for 30 minutes.

2. Cook the Filling:

- While the squash is baking, heat a skillet over medium heat.
- Add the chopped bacon to the skillet and cook for a few minutes until it starts to release its fat.
- Add the diced onion and chopped garlic to the skillet. Season with salt and pepper to taste. Continue to sauté for about 10 minutes, or until the onions are translucent and the bacon is crisp.
- Stir in the chopped spinach just before removing from heat. The residual heat will wilt the spinach.

3. Assemble and Finish Baking:

- After 30 minutes, remove the squash from the oven and carefully drain the water from the pan.
- Use tongs to flip the squash halves over so they are cut side up.
- Evenly distribute the bacon, onion, garlic, and spinach mixture into the cavities of the butternut squash halves.
- Sprinkle the mixed shredded cheese over the top of the filling in each squash half.
- Return the pan to the oven, now set at 250 degrees Fahrenheit (120 degrees Celsius), and bake for an additional 5 minutes, or until the cheese is melted and bubbly.

4. Serve:

- Remove the stuffed squash from the oven and let it cool slightly before serving.
- Serve hot, offering about 1 cup per serving as a satisfying main dish or a substantial side.

Macros (per serving):

- Net Carbs: 22g
- Fat: 33g
- Protein: 27g
- Serves 1 person

Preparation Time
45 minutes

Difficulty
normal

Grilled Asparagus

Ingredients:

- **1 pound of asparagus** - tough ends trimmed
- **8 teaspoons butter** - cut into small pieces (2 teaspoons per packet)
- **Cooking spray** - to coat the foil
- **1/2 teaspoon salt**
- **1/4 teaspoon pepper**
- **1 teaspoon Italian seasoning**
- **Lemon wedges** - for serving

- **For Baking:** Alternatively, if using an oven, place the foil packets on a baking sheet and bake for 15 minutes.

5. Finish and Serve:

- Carefully open the foil packets (watch out for the steam). Gently stir the asparagus within the packet to ensure all the stalks are evenly coated with the melted butter and seasonings.
- Serve immediately with lemon wedges for squeezing over the asparagus.

Macros (per serving):

- Net Carbs: 2g
- Fat: 8g
- Protein: 3g
- Serves: 4 person

Instructions:

1. Prepare the Asparagus:

- Preheat your grill to medium-high heat or your oven to 425 degrees Fahrenheit (220 degrees Celsius).
- Wash the asparagus and trim off the tough ends. If the stalks are very thick, you can peel the lower ends with a vegetable peeler for more even cooking.

2. Prepare the Foil Packets:

- Cut 4 large squares of aluminum foil and coat each square lightly with cooking spray.
- Divide the asparagus stalks evenly among the squares of foil.

3. Season the Asparagus:

- Sprinkle the Italian seasoning, salt, and pepper evenly over the asparagus stalks in each packet.
- Place 2 teaspoons of butter in small pieces over the asparagus in each packet.

4. Seal the Packets:

- Fold the foil over the asparagus, sealing the edges completely by crimping them together. Ensure the packets are sealed well so the butter and seasonings steam the asparagus as they cook.

5. Cook the Asparagus:

- **For Grilling:** Place the foil packets on the grill and cook for about 15 minutes, flipping once halfway through the cooking time.

Instructions:

1. For the vinaigrette

- In a mixing bowl, combine all the ingredients except the olive oil and whisk to combine. Slowly whisk in the olive oil until emulsified.

2. For the Brussels sprouts

- Preheat the oven to 400°F. Bring a large saucepan of salted water to a boil and prepare an ice bath. Working in batches, blanch the Brussels sprouts until almost tender, about 2 minutes. Transfer to the ice bath to cool, then transfer to paper towels and pat dry. Cut the Brussels sprouts in half.
- In a large ovenproof skillet, heat the oil over high heat until it shimmers. Add the Brussels sprouts, salt, and pepper and stir. Transfer to the oven and roast, stirring a few times, until the sprouts are well browned, 15–20 minutes.

3. For serving

- As soon as the Brussels sprouts come out of the oven, add the sunflower seeds and chile slices to the skillet and stir for a minute or so. Transfer to a serving platter or bowl. Top with the avocado and apple. Drizzle with the vinaigrette and top with the basil, mint, and some freshly grated lime zest. Season with flaky salt and pepper and serve.

CHEF'S TIP:

We talk a lot about balancing flavor and texture when creating new dishes, but I also like to consider temperature, specifically contrasting temperatures. There's something exciting about pairing hot and cold in a dish, like a drizzle of cool yogurt on a hot soup. Here, I pair roasted sprouts with cool, crisp apple and creamy avocado.

Ingredients:

Honey-Mustard Vinaigrette

- 2 tbsp fresh lime juice
- 2 tbsp fresh lemon juice
- 2 tbsp champagne vinegar
- 1 tsp honey
- 1½ tsp Dijon mustard
- ½ tsp wholegrain mustard
- ¾ tsp Tabasco hot sauce
- 1 tsp kosher salt
- 2 tbsp extra-virgin olive oil

Roasted Brussels Sprouts

- 1 pound Brussels sprouts, trimmed
- ¼ cup extra-virgin olive oil
- 1 tbsp kosher salt
- Freshly ground black pepper

For Serving

- Roasted Brussels sprouts
- 2 tbsp toasted sunflower seeds
- ½ red finger chile, thinly sliced (with seeds)
- ½ large avocado, cut into ½-inch cubes
- ½ Crispin or Golden Delicious apple (with skin), cored and cut in ½-inch cubes
- ¼ cup honey-mustard vinaigrette
- ½ cup roughly chopped basil
- ¼ cup roughly chopped mint
- 1 lime, for zesting
- Flaky salt and freshly ground black pepper

Macros (per serving):

- Net carbs: 6g
- Fat: 17g
- Protein: 4g
- Serves 4 people

Preparation Time
45 minutes

Difficulty
normal

Baked Salmon Over Mixed Greens

Ingredients:

- 16 oz. salmon (about 450 grams)
- 8 cups mixed greens
- 2 lemons, thinly sliced
- Salt and pepper to taste
- 6 tablespoons butter, melted
- 1 tablespoon honey
- 3 cloves garlic, minced
- 1 teaspoon fresh thyme leaves, chopped
- 1 teaspoon dried oregano
- Fresh parsley, for garnish
- Olive oil cooking spray (for greasing)

Instructions:

1. Preheat the Oven:

- Preheat your oven to 350°F (177°C). Line a large rimmed baking sheet with aluminum foil and lightly grease it with olive oil cooking spray.

2. Prepare the Salmon:

- Arrange the lemon slices in an even layer in the center of the prepared foil. This will act as a bed for the salmon, infusing it with lemony flavors as it cooks.
- Season both sides of the salmon fillets with salt and pepper, then place them on top of the lemon slices.

3. Make the Butter Mixture:

- In a small bowl, whisk together the melted butter, honey, minced garlic, chopped thyme, and dried oregano until well combined.

4. Bake the Salmon:

- Pour the butter mixture over the salmon. Fold the edges of the foil up around the salmon to create a sealed packet. This will help keep the moisture in and allow the salmon to steam in the butter mixture.
- Bake in the preheated oven for about 25 minutes, or until the salmon is cooked through and flakes easily with a fork.

5. Broil for Finishing:

- After baking, switch the oven to broil. Open the foil and broil the salmon for 2 minutes, or until the top gets slightly golden and the butter mixture thickens.

6. Serve:

- Place the mixed greens on plates. Top each bed of greens with a portion of the baked salmon.
- Garnish with fresh parsley to enhance the flavor and add a touch of color.

Macros (per serving):

- Net Carbs: 6g
- Fat: 32g
- Protein: 27g
- Serves: 4 person

Catfish with Olive Relish

Ingredients:

- 16 oz. catfish (cooked as desired)
- Grill seasoning to taste
- 1/2 cup olive oil, divided
- 4 small tomatoes or 1 large tomato, diced
- 1/4 cup chopped olives (choose your favorite type)
- Chives to taste, chopped
- 4 cups spinach, fresh
- 2 tablespoons olive oil (for sautéing spinach)

Macros (per serving):

- Net Carbs: 9g
- Fat: 26g
- Protein: 18g
- Serves: 4 person

Preparation Time
30 minutes

Difficulty
normal

Instructions:

1. Prepare the Olive Relish:

- In a mixing bowl, combine the grill seasoning with 1/3 cup of olive oil, chopped olives, and chives. Stir well to mix the ingredients thoroughly.

2. Sauté the Spinach:

- Heat the remaining 2 tablespoons of olive oil in a large skillet over medium heat. Add the spinach and sauté until it wilts and becomes tender, about 3-5 minutes. Set aside.

3. Combine Relish Ingredients:

- To the bowl with the olive mixture, add the diced tomatoes and sautéed spinach. Mix everything together until well combined.

4. Serve the Dish:

- Place the cooked catfish on a serving plate. Top the fish generously with the olive relish.

CHEF'S TIP:

This catfish with olive relish recipe offers a healthy balance of fats, protein, and carbs, making it an ideal choice for a fulfilling meal. The fresh flavors of the olives and tomatoes in the relish complement the richness of the fish beautifully, creating a dish that is as delicious as it is easy to prepare. Enjoy your meal, Marcos!

Coconut Fish Curry

Ingredients:

- 1/4 cup coconut oil
- 2 cups grape or cherry tomatoes, halved
- 2 cups fresh spinach leaves
- Salt and pepper to taste
- 4 pieces of fish (four-ounce each), such as mahi-mahi, mackerel, or grouper
- 2 teaspoons curry powder
- 1/2 cup coconut milk

Macros (per serving):

- Net Carbs: 6g
- Fat: 52g
- Protein: 48g
- Serves: 4 person

Preparation Time
20 minutes

Difficulty
normal

Instructions:

1. Cook Tomatoes:

- Heat the coconut oil in a large pan over medium heat. Add the halved tomatoes and cook for 4-6 minutes, or until they begin to blister and soften.

2. Add Spinach:

- To the pan with the tomatoes, add the spinach leaves. Cook for an additional 4-5 minutes, stirring frequently, until the spinach is wilted. Season with salt and pepper to taste, then remove the mixture from the pan and set aside.

3. Season and Cook the Fish:

- Season the fish pieces with salt and pepper on both sides.
- In the same pan used for the tomatoes and spinach, place the fish. Cook for about 4 minutes on one side if the pieces are about 1 inch thick.

4. Add Curry Powder and Coconut Milk:

- Flip the fish over. Sprinkle the curry powder over the fish, then pour in the coconut milk. Cook for another 4 minutes, or until the fish is fully cooked through and the sauce has slightly thickened.

5. Serve:

- Plate the fish by placing the spinach and tomato mixture on a serving dish first, then topping it with the cooked fish. Drizzle any remaining sauce from the pan over the top.

Cod with Hazelnut Sauce & Asparagus

Ingredients:

- 16 oz. cod fillet (cut into 4 pieces)
- 1/4 cup grass-fed butter
- 1/2 cup roasted hazelnuts, chopped
- Fresh lemon juice (from about 1 lemon)
- 2 bunches of asparagus spears, roasted (approximately 8 cups)
- Salt and pepper, to taste

Macros (per serving):

- Net Carbs: 2g
- Fat: 33g
- Protein: 21g
- Serves: 4 person

Preparation Time
25 minutes

Difficulty
normal

Instructions:

1. Preheat and Prepare Asparagus:

- Preheat your oven to 400°F (200°C). Trim the ends of the asparagus spears, toss them with a little olive oil, salt, and pepper, and arrange them in a single layer on a baking sheet. Roast in the oven for about 12-15 minutes until tender and slightly caramelized.

2. Cook the Cod:

- In a large skillet, heat the butter over medium heat until melted and foamy. Season the cod fillets with salt and pepper, and place them in the skillet. Cook for about 2 minutes on one side until golden.

3. Add Hazelnuts and Lemon Juice:

- Flip the cod fillets over. Add the chopped hazelnuts around the cod in the pan. Squeeze fresh lemon juice over the cod and hazelnuts. Cook for another 2-3 minutes, or until the cod is cooked through and the hazelnuts are fragrant.

4. Serve:

- Plate the roasted asparagus on a serving dish. Top with the cod fillets. Spoon the buttery hazelnut and lemon sauce from the pan over the cod and asparagus.

Grilled Trout with Dill Sauce

Ingredients:

- 16 oz. trout, cut into 4 pieces
- Salt and pepper, to taste
- 1/2 cup mayonnaise
- 4 teaspoons mustard
- 1/2 cup fresh dill, chopped
- Juice of 2 lemons
- 1 cup carrots, shredded
- 2 cups string beans
- 1/2 cup water
- 3/8 cup almonds, toasted

Macros (per serving):

- Net Carbs: 6g
- Fat: 28g
- Protein: 10g
- Serves: 4 person

Preparation Time
20 minutes

Difficulty
normal

Instructions:

1. Prepare the Grill:
- Heat a grill pan over medium heat and coat it with cooking spray.

2. Grill the Trout:
- Place the trout pieces on the grill pan. Cook on one side for 2-3 minutes.
- Flip the trout, season with salt and pepper, and cover. Cook for another 3-4 minutes or until the trout is cooked through. Remove from pan and set aside

3. Cook the Vegetables:
- In the same pan, add the shredded carrots and string beans along with 1/2 cup of water. Cook until the vegetables reach your desired tenderness, seasoning with salt and pepper as needed.

4. Make the Dill Sauce:
- In a small bowl, whisk together the mayonnaise, mustard, chopped dill, and lemon juice until well combined.

5. Serve:
- Plate the grilled trout on top of the cooked string beans and carrots.
- Sprinkle the trout with toasted almonds.
- Serve the dill sauce on the side for drizzling or dipping.

Herb Salmon with Roasted Asparagus

Ingredients:

- 4 ounces salmon
- Fresh herbs of choice (such as dill, parsley, thyme)
- 1 cup asparagus, trimmed
- 2 tablespoons olive oil
- 1 teaspoon sesame seeds
- Salt and pepper, to taste

Macros (per serving):

- Net Carbs: 3g
- Fat: 45g
- Protein: 29g
- Serves: 1 person

Preparation Time
30 minutes

Difficulty
normal

Instructions:

1. Poach the Salmon:

- Fill a skillet with enough water to cover the salmon and bring it to a gentle simmer.
- Add your chosen fresh herbs to the water to infuse it with flavor.
- Place the salmon in the simmering water, making sure it is submerged. Poach the salmon for about 10-15 minutes or until it is cooked through and flakes easily.

2. Prepare and Roast the Asparagus:

- Preheat your oven to 350°F (175°C).
- Toss the asparagus spears with 2 tablespoons of olive oil, and season with salt and pepper.
- Spread the asparagus in a single layer on a baking sheet. Roast in the preheated oven for 25-30 minutes, until tender and slightly caramelized.

3. Finish the Asparagus:

- Once roasted, remove the asparagus from the oven and toss with sesame seeds.

4. Serve:

- Arrange the poached salmon on a plate alongside the roasted asparagus spears.

High Heat Roasted Fish and Vegetables

Ingredients:

- 1/2 cup coconut oil, melted
- 1 cup butternut squash, cut into 1/2-inch cubes
- 2 cups Brussels sprouts, trimmed and halved
- 4 pieces (four ounces each) of fish, such as halibut, mahi-mahi, or cod
- 1/2 teaspoon salt, plus extra to taste
- 1/2 teaspoon pepper, plus extra to taste
- 1/2 teaspoon fresh thyme
- 1 lemon, quartered
- 3 tablespoons pumpkin seeds

- Serve each portion with a lemon wedge to squeeze over the fish for added zest.

Macros (per serving):

- Net Carbs: 7g
- Fat: 32g
- Protein: 29g
- Serves: 4 person

Preparation Time
30 minutes

Difficulty
normal

Instructions:

1. Preheat the Oven:

- Preheat your oven to 425°F (220°C). This high temperature is key for achieving perfectly roasted vegetables and a nicely cooked fish.

2. Prepare the Vegetables:

- In a large bowl, toss the melted coconut oil with the butternut squash and Brussels sprouts. Season with salt and pepper to taste.
- Spread the vegetables in a single layer on a large baking sheet, ensuring they are not overcrowded to allow for even roasting.

3. Prepare and Season the Fish:

- Place the fish fillets on top of the vegetables on the baking sheet. Make sure to leave some space between each piece to ensure even cooking.
- Season the fish fillets with salt, pepper, and fresh thyme.

4. Roast:

- Place the tray in the preheated oven and roast for about 15 minutes, or until the fish flakes easily with a fork and the vegetables are tender and caramelized.

5. Serve:

- Remove from the oven and immediately plate the fish and vegetables.
- Sprinkle pumpkin seeds over the top for added texture and a slight nutty flavor.

Cod with Hazelnut Sauce & Asparagus

Ingredients:

- 16 oz. cod fillet (cut into 4 pieces)
- 1/4 cup grass-fed butter
- 1/2 cup roasted hazelnuts, chopped
- Fresh lemon juice (from about 1 lemon)
- 2 bunches of asparagus spears, roasted (approximately 8 cups)
- Salt and pepper, to taste

Macros (per serving):

- Net Carbs: 2g
- Fat: 33g
- Protein: 21g
- Serves: 4 person

Preparation Time
25 minutes

Difficulty
normal

Instructions:

1. Preheat and Prepare Asparagus:
- Preheat your oven to 400°F (200°C). Trim the ends of the asparagus spears, toss them with a little olive oil, salt, and pepper, and arrange them in a single layer on a baking sheet. Roast in the oven for about 12-15 minutes until tender and slightly caramelized.

2. Cook the Cod:
- In a large skillet, heat the butter over medium heat until melted and foamy. Season the cod fillets with salt and pepper, and place them in the skillet. Cook for about 2 minutes on one side until golden.

3. Add Hazelnuts and Lemon Juice:
- Flip the cod fillets over. Add the chopped hazelnuts around the cod in the pan. Squeeze fresh lemon juice over the cod and hazelnuts. Cook for another 2-3 minutes, or until the cod is cooked through and the hazelnuts are fragrant.

4. Serve:
- Plate the roasted asparagus on a serving dish. Top with the cod fillets. Spoon the buttery hazelnut and lemon sauce from the pan over the cod and asparagus.

Grilled Trout with Dill Sauce

Ingredients:

- 16 oz. trout, cut into 4 pieces
- Salt and pepper, to taste
- 1/2 cup mayonnaise
- 4 teaspoons mustard
- 1/2 cup fresh dill, chopped
- Juice of 2 lemons
- 1 cup carrots, shredded
- 2 cups string beans
- 1/2 cup water
- 3/8 cup almonds, toasted

Macros (per serving):

- Net Carbs: 6g
- Fat: 28g
- Protein: 10g
- Serves: 4 person

Preparation Time
20 minutes

Difficulty
normal

Instructions:

1. Prepare the Grill:

- Heat a grill pan over medium heat and coat it with cooking spray.

2. Grill the Trout:

- Place the trout pieces on the grill pan. Cook on one side for 2-3 minutes.
- Flip the trout, season with salt and pepper, and cover. Cook for another 3-4 minutes or until the trout is cooked through. Remove from pan and set aside.

3. Cook the Vegetables:

- In the same pan, add the shredded carrots and string beans along with 1/2 cup of water. Cook until the vegetables reach your desired tenderness, seasoning with salt and pepper as needed

4. Make the Dill Sauce:

- In a small bowl, whisk together the mayonnaise, mustard, chopped dill, and lemon juice until well combined.

5. Serve:

- Plate the grilled trout on top of the cooked string beans and carrots.
- Sprinkle the trout with toasted almonds.
- Serve the dill sauce on the side for drizzling or dipping.

Herb Salmon with Roasted Asparagus

Ingredients:

- 4 ounces salmon
- Fresh herbs of choice (such as dill, parsley, thyme)
- 1 cup asparagus spears
- 2 tablespoons olive oil
- 1 teaspoon sesame seeds
- Salt and pepper, to taste

Macros (per serving):

- Net Carbs: 3g
- Fat: 45g
- Protein: 29g
- Serves: 1 person

Preparation Time
30 minutes

Difficulty
normal

Instructions:

1. Poach the Salmon:

- Fill a skillet with enough water to just cover the salmon. Bring to a gentle simmer.
- Add a generous amount of fresh herbs to the water to infuse it with flavor.
- Gently place the salmon in the simmering water, ensuring it is submerged. Poach the salmon for about 10-15 minutes, or until it is cooked through and easily flakes with a fork. Remove from water and set aside.

2. Prepare and Roast the Asparagus:

- Preheat your oven to 350°F (175°C).
- Toss the asparagus spears with olive oil, and season with salt and pepper.
- Spread the asparagus on a baking sheet in a single layer. Roast in the preheated oven for 25-30 minutes, until tender and lightly browned.

3. Serve:

- Remove the asparagus from the oven and toss with sesame seeds.
- Arrange the asparagus on a plate and place the poached salmon alongside.

High Heat Roasted Fish and Vegetables

Ingredients:

- 1/2 cup coconut oil, melted
- 1 cup butternut squash, cut into 1/2-inch cubes
- 2 cups Brussels sprouts, trimmed and halved
- 4 pieces (four ounces each) of fish, such as halibut, mahi-mahi, or cod
- 1/2 teaspoon salt, plus extra to taste
- 1/2 teaspoon pepper, plus extra to taste
- 1/2 teaspoon fresh thyme
- 1 lemon, quartered
- 3 tablespoons pumpkin seeds

Macros (per serving):

- Net Carbs: 7g
- Fat: 32g
- Protein: 29g
- Serves: 1 person

Preparation Time
30 minutes

Difficulty
normal

Instructions:

1. Preheat the Oven:

- Preheat your oven to 425°F (220°C). This high temperature is key for achieving perfectly roasted vegetables and nicely cooked fish.

2. Prepare the Vegetables:

- In a large bowl, toss the melted coconut oil with the butternut squash and Brussels sprouts. Season with salt and pepper.
- Spread the vegetables in a single layer on a large baking sheet, ensuring they are not overcrowded to allow for even roasting

3. Prepare and Season the Fish:

- Place the fish fillets on top of the vegetables on the baking sheet. Make sure to leave some space between each piece to ensure even cooking.
- Season the fish fillets with salt, pepper, and fresh thyme.

4. Roast:

- Place the tray in the preheated oven and roast for about 15 minutes, or until the fish flakes easily with a fork and the vegetables are tender and caramelized.

5. Serve:

- Remove from the oven and immediately plate the fish and vegetables.
- Sprinkle pumpkin seeds over the top for added texture and a slight nutty flavor.

Shrimp Scampi

Ingredients:

- **12 oz raw shrimp, peeled and deveined** - The star of the dish.
- **1/4 cup olive oil -** Used for cooking and flavoring.
- **1/4 cup butter** - Adds richness to the sauce.
- **4 cloves garlic, minced** - Provides a robust flavor.
- **4 cups zucchini, spiralized** - A healthy, low-carb alternative to pasta.
- **Lemon juice** - To taste, for brightness.
- **Parsley** - To taste, for garnish and added flavor.
- **Red pepper flakes, salt, and pepper** - To taste, for seasoning.

Optional:

- **1 cup cooked broccoli** - Adds extra nutrients and texture.
- **1 tablespoon olive oil** - For dressing the broccoli.
- **2 tablespoons ground flaxseed** - For an added boost of fiber and omega-3 fatty acids.

Instructions:

1. Prepare the Shrimp:

- Heat a large pan over medium heat.
- Add the shrimp and ⅓ cup of water to the pan. Sauté until the shrimp turn pink and are cooked through, about 2-3 minutes per side, depending on the size of the shrimp. Remove the shrimp from the pan and set aside.

2. Make the Sauce:

- In the same pan, reduce the heat to medium-low and add the olive oil, butter, minced garlic, and red pepper flakes. Stir to combine and allow the butter to melt completely, infusing the oil with garlic and spices. Season with salt and pepper to taste.

3. Cook the Zucchini Noodles:

- Add the spiralized zucchini to the pan. Cook for a few minutes, stirring occasionally, until the noodles are tender but still hold their shape. The exact cooking time will depend on your preference for noodle texture.

4. Combine and Finish:

- Return the cooked shrimp to the pan with the zucchini noodles. Drizzle with lemon juice and sprinkle with chopped parsley. Stir everything together to combine well and reheat the shrimp.

5. Serve:

- Plate the shrimp scampi and zucchini noodles immediately. Serve hot.

Optional:

- If including broccoli, toss the cooked broccoli with 1 tablespoon olive oil and 2 tablespoons ground flaxseed. Serve alongside or mixed into the shrimp scampi.

Macros (per serving):

- Net Carbs: 6g (excluding optional ingredients)
- Fat: Varied, depending on the use of butter and olive oil
- Protein: High, primarily from shrimp
- Serves: 4 person

Preparation Time
20 minutes

Difficulty
normal

Citrus Avocado Salad

Ingredients:

For the Salad:

- **1 grapefruit**, peeled and segmented - Adds a sweet and slightly tangy flavor.
- **1 orange**, peeled and segmented - Provides sweetness and juiciness.
- **1 Meyer lemon**, peeled and segmented - Brings a distinct, sweet citrus note.
- **1 avocado**, thinly sliced - Offers a creamy texture and rich flavor.
- **Quick pickled onions**, for topping - Adds a sharp, tangy contrast.

For the Honey Lime Vinaigrette:

- **2 tablespoons freshly squeezed lime juice** - The acidic base of the dressing.
- **1 1/2 tablespoons honey** - For sweetness and to balance the acidity.
- **1 garlic clove, minced** - Adds a punch of flavor.
- **1 pinch salt and pepper** - For seasoning.
- **3 tablespoons olive oil** - Helps emulsify the dressing and adds smoothness.

Instructions

1. Prepare the Citrus:

- Segment the grapefruit, orange, and Meyer lemon. To do this, cut off the top and bottom of each fruit so they sit flat. Using a knife, follow the curve of the fruit to remove the skin and white pith. Over a bowl, cut between the membranes to release the segments.

2. Prepare the Avocado:

- Cut the avocado in half and remove the pit. Peel the skin or scoop the avocado out with a spoon. Slice the avocado thinly.

3. Assemble the Salad:

- On a serving plate, arrange the citrus segments and avocado slices aesthetically. Scatter the quick onions over the top. Sprinkle a little salt and pepper over the salad to enhance the flavors.

4. Make the Honey Lime Vinaigrette:

- In a small bowl, whisk together the lime juice, honey, minced garlic, salt, and pepper until well combined.
- Continue whisking while gradually adding the olive oil to ensure the dressing emulsifies and becomes somewhat thick.

5. Dress the Salad:

- Drizzle the Honey Lime Vinaigrette over the arranged salad just before serving to ensure the avocado and citrus don't become soggy.

6. Serve:

- Serve the salad immediately to enjoy the fresh and crisp textures, complemented by the sweet and tangy dressing.

Macros (per serving):

- Net Carbs: Approximately 15g per serving, mainly from the fruits and honey.
- Fat: Healthy fats primarily from the avocado and olive oil.
- Protein: Minimal; this dish is more focused on healthy fats and vitamin
- Serves: 2-4 person

Preparation Time

20 minutes

Difficulty

easy

CHAPTER THREE
SPEAK

Embarking on a journey like the Galveston Diet can be an exhilarating yet challenging adventure. As you navigate through the highs and lows, it's essential to recognize that weight loss and health improvement are not linear processes. This realization can fuel your motivation and help you persist, even when progress seems elusive.

Firstly, understand that fluctuations in weight are entirely normal. Many factors can affect your weight on a daily basis, including water retention, hormonal changes, and even the amount of sleep you get. When you step on the scale and see a number that discourages you, remember that it's not just about fat loss but about overall health and well-being.

During the tough weeks when the scale doesn't budge or when you find yourself resisting your favorite unhealthy snacks without immediate reward, it's crucial to stay focused on your long-term goals. These moments of resistance are actually strengthening your willpower and helping you build a healthier relationship with food.

The concept of the "LISTENING TO MY BODY" effect—as frustrating as it might be—teaches us patience. It's a reminder that sometimes our bodies need time to adjust and recalibrate. This adjustment period is a critical part of the weight loss journey. Just as the body takes time to accumulate fat, it also takes time to lose it sustainably.

To keep your spirits high, celebrate every small victory along the way. Did you choose a healthy lunch over fast food? That's a win. Managed a 30-minute walk even though you felt like skipping it? Another win. These choices add up and significantly impact your health over time.

Moreover, diversify your sources of motivation. While weight loss can be a powerful initial motivator, focusing too exclusively on the scale can lead to frustration. Instead, pay attention to how you feel. Are you more energetic? Do your clothes fit better? Is your skin clearer? These are all signs that you're on the right track.

Creating a supportive environment can also greatly enhance your perseverance. Surround yourself with people who understand and support your goals. If possible, join communities—either online or in real life—of like-minded individuals who are also on their own health journeys. Sharing experiences and tips can provide not just support but also new strategies that might work better for you.

Setbacks are inevitable, but each one is an opportunity to learn and grow. If you find yourself giving in to an old habit, reflect on what led to that decision. Understanding your triggers can help you create strategies to avoid them in the future.

Moreover, incorporate flexibility into your diet plan. The Galveston Diet, like any diet, is a guideline—not a strict rulebook. If you find certain aspects of the diet too challenging, adapt it to fit your needs better. This might mean adjusting your eating windows, tweaking your macros, or finding healthier alternatives to favored dishes that still satisfy your cravings.

Education is also key. The more you understand about nutrition and how your body works, the more empowered you'll feel to make informed decisions. This might involve reading up on the latest diet science, understanding the role of different nutrients, or even learning how to cook new, healthy recipes.

Lastly, remember why you started. Write down your reasons for embarking on this diet and read them when you're feeling low. Whether it's for health reasons, to improve your self-esteem, or to achieve a long-term goal, keeping these reasons in mind can give you the extra push you need to keep going.

Thank You

"The journey through the Galveston Diet or any health improvement plan is full of ups and downs. By maintaining focus on your overall well-being, celebrating small successes, learning from setbacks, and understanding your body's natural rhythms, you can sustain motivation and continue moving towards a healthier you. Stay patient, stay flexible, and, most importantly, stay committed. Your health is worth every effort".

Printed in Great Britain
by Amazon